Seeing Heaven
From Planet Earth

DIANE EHRLICH

REFORM MINISTRY PUBLICATIONS

ISBN: 979-8-218-26804-6

Scripture quotations are taken from *The Holy Bible New International Version*, © 1973, 1978, 1984 by The International Bible Society, used by permission.

Scripture quotations are taken from the *New American Standard Bible*, © 1960, 1962, 1963, 1971, 1973, 1975, 1977, The Lockman Foundation, used by permission.

Published by Reform Ministry Publications
Cleveland, Ohio
www.reformministry.com

"So we fix our eyes not on what is seen, but on what is unseen. For what is seen is temporary, but what is unseen is eternal."

2 Corinthians 4:18

TABLE OF CONTENTS

FROM THE AUTHOR

I wanted to write a book that people would remember. Of all the books that people are reading, I wanted mine to stand out for its charm. Using the writing method of simile i.e., this is like that, I wrote a collection of symbolic comparisons called parables.

Parables are pictorial stories about familiar objects crafted to introduce spiritual principles. They are meant to captivate the imagination by providing something recognizable and linking it to the unknown. Through them, people can envision the unseen realm of God.

This devotional book resulted from my original blogs posted on my Reform Ministry website, www.reformministry.com. By tracking visitors to the website, I was amazed to find that people across the country and even around the world read my blogs! Every month, engaging articles were offered with personal stories and corresponding photos. Soon, I had enough material to create this book.

My husband, Barry, retired me from my full-time job so that I would have time to write. He is the subject of many of the articles and I can't thank him enough for his loving support. He is my sounding board, and I am grateful for his feedback as he carefully listened to each of my drafts.

I also want to thank my marketing coach, Dave Van Horn and The Cleveland Writers Group Meetup, for first suggesting the blog-to-book idea. Together they have given me valuable guidance to complete my projects and advance my marketing goals.

Many thanks to my initial proofreaders Gerry Siefert, Madison Chakey and William Chakey for their important candid comments. I am also grateful to professional editor Brett Kinsey / The Freelance Editor LLC www.TheFreelanceEditors.com for helping to make my writing stronger. Thanks to everyone involved who invested themselves in this piece.

All this to the glory of God! As you read, I hope you gain a fuller understanding of heaven through these parables!

INTRODUCTION

*L*ike the reflection of sun-kissed clouds mirrored onto a lake below, we can see heaven reflected in things on earth. This "seeing" is not physical sight, but rather understanding that comes from picturing in our mind. Then we have snapshots into God's unseen realm, and it remedies some of the mystery. Greater familiarity with God inches us closer to Him.

Our belief in God and in heaven is not untethered. This fantastic realm has not been relinquished to vivid human imaginations. We can know attributes of heaven from God's vantage point rather than just guessing.

The Bible gives ample information about the character of God, glimpses of His dwelling place, and knowledge of the afterlife. The historical account of the nation Israel culminating in the ministry of Jesus is the basis for doctrine that is real and true.

Center stage is God the Father revealing Himself in Jesus the Son. Jesus stated, **"If you have seen Me, then you have seen the Father."** **(John 14:9)** He amplified this by saying, **"I and the Father are one."** **(John 10:30)** Everything that Jesus taught about God and the heavenly realm came from His first-hand knowledge. Jesus spoke with authority because He described what He knew.

"The Kingdom of God is like…" This was the iconic phrase that Jesus used to teach the multitudes. The parables of Jesus recorded in the Gospels were simple, yet compelling stories crafted to bring His followers to spiritual enlightenment. The purpose of the parables was to guide listeners to reach a moral conclusion. This was a discreet appeal to human logic using hypothetical situations that pressed listeners to moralize about their own choices. Rather than speak directly, i.e., "You should do this," the parable allowed individuals to reason out their own choice, i.e., "I should do this." Then they would own their choice. Overall, the parables were meant to locate people and urge them to align themselves with the standards of heaven.

The crowds were receptive to Jesus' teaching style and many concluded that He was the Son of God. **"Jesus spoke all these things to the crowd in parables; he did not say anything to them without using a parable. So was fulfilled what was spoken through the prophet: 'I will open my mouth in parables, I will** utter things hidden since the creation of the world.'" (Matthew 13: 34-35)

Teaching with parables was not exclusive to Jesus. Ancient rhetorical writings were often used in Buddhism and in Chinese culture. Later in history, Greek mythology incorporated fictitious stories or legends to explain occurrences in nature. [1]

Old Testament Jewish history was the primary influence for Jesus' use of parables. He learned this style from Old Testament books such as Job, the Psalms, Ezekiel, Micah, and Habakkuk. **"Now the word of the Lord came to me saying, 'Son of man, propound a riddle, and speak a parable to the house of Israel.'" (Ezekiel 17: 1-2)**

Persuasive speech using parables did not originate with Jesus, but He undeniably mastered it. His stories were effective because they helped people envision what heaven was like. **"And He said, 'How shall we picture the kingdom of God, or by what parable shall we present it? It is like..." (Mark 4:30-31)** The parables of Jesus are among the best known, most influential stories in the world. He knew that, apart from personal experience, stories were the quickest way to learn. [2] Ideally, if people could catch a glimpse of heaven, they would do whatever it took to obtain it for themselves, above all other acquisitions. Through preaching, teaching, and performing miracles, Jesus was on a mission to point people to God and offer them heaven.

The efficiency of stories combined with moral teaching is the essence of this devotional. Describing familiar items from everyday life to

---

1. *Stories With Intent*, P. 4
2. Ibid, P. 1

point to their heavenly counterparts is this book's main theme. Pictures combined with words is a doubly effective tool as the mind connects the two. Hopefully, the word pictures and corresponding scriptures will stick with you as you remember the visuals.

As you read, perhaps a story each day, you will be investing in your spiritual life. Read the suggested scripture reference as a basis for each lesson. You can participate by jotting down your thoughts in the space provided at the end. You may draw conclusions that are different than mine. How wonderful is that?

Most importantly, I pray that this reading experience will inspire you to be a more passionate follower of Jesus, ready for His service. May Christ richly bless you as you open yourself to His Word.

"Z" IS FOR "ZUCCHINI"

READ MATTHEW 19: 27-30

Z ucchinis are weird looking vegetables, growing out from the bottom of the plant stem, topped by a golden star-like flower. They remind me of the long, stretchy balloons that clowns blow up and twist together at carnivals to create hats or replicas of wiener dogs! Zucchini plants command the vegetable patch with large, brilliant emerald-green leaves, ruffled and lush, that shade the underlying vegetables. If you have never seen them growing, I hope my description helps you envision them.

"Z" is for "zucchini." Traditional phonetics may teach "Z" stands for "zebra." But I needed a picture for my blog post, and I have zucchini plants growing in my garden, not zebras. The letter "Z" is the last letter of the English alphabet but has comparatively few words beginning with it. That does not diminish its value, though. Without it, we would not have the words "fuzzy," "dizzy," and "bamboozle." The letter "Z" is equal to all the other letters because it helps make our language colorful and complete. Concerning the letters of the alphabet, the last is just as important as the first.

That was the issue when the Disciples asked Jesus what their eternal reward would be for their great sacrifice of leaving their farms and families to preach the Kingdom. Curiously, He answered them with a riddle. **"But many who are first will be last and the last, first."** **(Matthew 19:30)** He further explained with the parable of the workers in the field.

The story described a landowner who hired workers to work in his field. Some were hired early in the morning, while others were hired late in the day. At the end of the shift, all the workers received the same pay no matter how long they worked. "Unfair!" The first workers objected. The landowner answered them with this reasoning. **"'Friend, I am doing you no wrong; did you not agree with me for a denarius? Take what is yours and go your way, but I wish to give to this man the same as to you. Is it not lawful for me to do what I wish with what is my own? Or is your eye envious because I am generous?' Thus, the last shall be first and the first last."** (Matthew 20:13-16)

Perhaps Jesus left the Disciples scratching their heads, still wondering what He meant. We now have the fullness of scripture to understand His teaching. Just like "the last shall be first," His message lifted the hope of the masses that they would not be discounted by God because of their downtrodden conditions. All servants of God are equally valued by Him with no one having greater status. The Sermon on the Mount also clashed with the norms of culture. **"Blessed are the poor in spirit for theirs is the Kingdom of God." (Matthew 5:3)** He gave people hope that the unfair economic system favoring the Roman ruling class would someday be abolished. The Kingdom of God had a different standard where humility, gentleness and mercy are currency. He assured them that there is a blessedness in following God for those who will wait for His Kingdom. God Himself will be the sole landowner of the world and He will institute justice ad equity.

When that happens, all people will be uplifted and esteemed by God, not based on works, wealth, or class. To answer the Disciples' question, Christian sacrifice will be then be honored as acts of love and obedience to God for all to see and appreciate.

Using our alphabet analogy, someday there will be no big "I's" and little "U's." God will rule justly. The weak will not be oppressed, and the powerful will not have preferential treatment. Human rights will finally be upheld.

To answer the "not fair" objection in the parable, there is nothing fair about God's generosity to us through grace. Grace is the system of justice that Jesus afforded a world that was estranged from God by sin. At Christ's expense, the debt of sin was paid, its death sentence carried out to God's perfect satisfaction.

There will be nothing fair about the Apostle Paul, a zealous religious murderer who by his own admission was the worst of sinners, standing at the final judgment alongside a lifelong Sunday school teacher who accepted God's forgiveness as a teen at a youth retreat. This is not "apples to apples" fair, but they will both be there because of God's grace.

Therefore, if the last are first or the first are last, it doesn't matter because God's grace blankets all who believe in Him and receive Him. Christ is the greatest reward and ultimate prize to obtain. Those whose hearts are penetrated by the parables will make the connection. Heaven will be completely and colorfully populated by grateful forgiven people, A to Z, from every tongue, tribe, and nation. And none of them gazing into the loving eyes of Jesus will be thinking about big "I's" and little "U's."

YOUR THOUGHTS

ALL MEN ARE LIKE GRASS

READ ISAIAH 40: 6-11

*M*y grandfather Bill Myers was a seasoned gardener, raised on a farm in southern Ohio. He came north to the Cleveland area along with my grandmother to teach school, specializing in American history. After retirement, he focused on raising an expansive garden, plowing up the fertile soil with his tractor disk every spring. Normally he planted two fields of sweetcorn, maneuvering his tractor over a makeshift bridge to cross a drainage creek that divided the land into front garden and back garden.

He strategically placed scarecrows on wooden posts in the fields, tying aluminum pie pans on them to scare the birds with movement and noise. He stuffed his old work shirts with straw to make the scarecrows look and smell more human. I'm not sure if the crows really caught on. As kids, if we saw a flock of birds pecking seed in the garden, we would run and scare them away. When we visited my grandparents, *we became* the scarecrows!

The corn and bean plants were also vulnerable to the appetites of raccoons and rabbits. Eventually the harvest of corn, beans, peas, squash, Swiss chard, and kohlrabi was plentiful, even after a season's battle with critters.

With the picture of scarecrows in mind, let's segue to the Bible where God speaks through the prophet Isaiah and says, **"All flesh is like grass..."** (Isaiah 40:6) The scripture continues by saying that the glory of people quickly fades like grass and wilts like a field flower. **"The grass withers and the flower fades..."** (Isaiah 40:8)

This is meant to highlight the brevity of human life and the fading beauty of youth, putting life in perspective. This does not mean that our lives are inconsequential. Some people accomplish much within the span of the decades they have. There is a glory in attaining influence and success, just like my grandfather did with hundreds of students over the years.

The next sentence of the scripture brings the meaning into focus. **"But the word of our God stands forever."** (Isaiah 40:8) Every person's life is blink-of-an-eye brief in comparison to the enduring Word of God. Century after century, the glory of God's Word never fades, never becomes less potent, is never less true and is always relevant.

In the parable of the sower, Jesus explains the Word of God as a seed planted within the soil of the human heart. He tells His Disciples, **"Now the parable is this: the seed is the word of God." (Luke 8:11)** He speaks of different types of soil that represent the many heart postures of people. Some have rocky soil that is shallow and hard. Others are thorny from the all-consuming cares of life. And others are good fertile soil, like my grandfather's garden, that easily receives the seed and produces a crop of right living. **"And the seed in the good soil, those are the ones who have heard the word in an honest and good heart, and hold it fast, and bear fruit with perseverance." (Luke 8:15)** Holding fast is an expression of resolute belief when people internalize the word and act upon its values.

This picture is further developed by the Apostle Peter as he teaches about the supernatural quality of God's Word. **"For you have been born again not of seed which is perishable but imperishable, that is, through the living and abiding word of God." (1 Peter 1:22-23)** He quotes our reference verse in Isaiah 40 to ground his teaching to the prophet.

God's Word, the Bible, is living and active, able to locate us and change us. By reading it, we can understand what God is like, realize what Jesus has done and have the New Testament revelations to teach us godly living. In the brief season of our lives, we can have a "crop" of the knowledge of God's will, resulting in new life and good works that are beneficial and consequential.

YOUR THOUGHTS

HUGADAY

READ PROVERBS 8:22-31

"*H*UGADAY." Those were the letters of a license plate on the back of a white Buick in the parking lot.

"*People are so creative,*" I thought to myself.

Seeing the letters made me feel like the owner wanted to spread verbal hugs, however fleeting, to other drivers. Motorists could stop at a red light behind this vehicle, decipher the letters and grin to themselves as the light turned green! I was charmed by this person's gracious public gesture and immediately became a fan of random hugs.

Hugs are easy to give and receive. Handshakes are friendly but formal. Kisses are way too intimate. But hugs land in the middle as appropriate, healthy behavior. People don't have to find words when they hug others because body language speaks for itself. It says, "I want to be close to you." I believe those who hug necks freely are free people who understand the value of dispensing doses of emotional medicine.

I think of "hugaday" when I consider God's ability to be there for each of us every single day. Jesus promised to be with us in this age and forever. **"I am with you always, even to the end of the age."** **(Matthew 28:20)** He is always available to us. No day goes by without access to God's love, power, and mercy.

Solomon, the author of Proverbs, expressed this easy access to God by creating the persona, Wisdom. Disguised as a witness to the magnitude of creation, Wisdom speaks in first person, but is actually the mind of God speaking for Himself. **"When He marked out the foundations of the earth; Then I was beside Him, as a master workman. And I was daily His delight, rejoicing always before Him, rejoicing in the world, His earth, and delighting in mankind."** **(Proverbs 8:30-31)** From this passage, we get a panoramic view of God's creative power at work, the heavenly bodies, the earth, and humankind. As He scans His creation, He delights in it and especially in us.

From the position of eternal love, God sees every person on the planet every day, every hour, and every moment...all at once. We are never not in His view. **"For the eyes of the Lord range throughout the earth to strengthen those whose hearts are fully committed to Him."** **(2 Chronicles 16:9)** In the musings of Job we read this:

"His eyes are on the ways of man; he sees their every step..." (Job 34:21) The Psalmist personalizes God's omniscience even more. **"You know when I sit and when I stand...Before a word is on my tongue you know it completely." (Psalm 139:104)** The full scope of this ongoing scrutiny is unknowable to man, yet consoling because we know that His gaze is benevolent.

Finally, here is the "hug" part as God presents Himself as Savior to lift our burdens from us. **"Praise be to the Lord, to our Savior who daily bears our burdens." (Psalm 68:19)** God sustains His world and He sustains us. His heavenly hug comes from His personal intervention. This is the hope that we all can have: **"You who seek God, may your hearts live!" (Psalm 69:32)** Look to Him and expect a "hugaday" that your heart may live!

YOUR THOUGHTS

_____
_____
_____
_____
_____
_____
_____
_____
_____
_____
_____
_____
_____
_____
_____
_____
_____
_____
_____
_____
_____

SUNNY SIDE UP

READ NUMBERS 6:22-27

*M*y husband Barry has a great sense of humor! One Sunday morning I thought of placing two sunny side up eggs and some bacon into a frying pan to make a "Smiley Face" for my monthly blog. I decided to use his breakfast for the picture!

He gladly indulged me. As he helped me position the food and snap a couple of photos with my phone, his eggs grew cold. He ate them anyway, fingerprints and all without complaining, giving me another reason to be glad I married him.

He tells me all the time that people say he should do stand-up comedy. He says he loves to make people laugh. On those occasions, I strike a dramatic pose, pretend to faint, and say, "Please don't quit your day job or we shall be ruined!" I figure he has enough unsuspecting customers at the hardware store where he works to practice his jokes on. Who knows? Maybe someday a Hollywood scout will come into the store to buy duct tape, and he will be discovered!

Even so, my funny man has a serious side to him. One time when he was walking to his car, he spotted a lady near him who was standing in the parking lot staring into space. He got her attention by saying, "Pardon me. Are you alright?"

She shook her head and said, "No. I was just diagnosed with breast cancer." Then she caught herself. "I can't believe I just told you that!" she said.

Barry felt the Spirit of God prompt him to ask her, "Would you like me to pray with you?" She agreed and he followed the lead of the Holy Spirit to give him the words to pray for this troubled lady. After praying, he consoled her by saying, "You will find support in the Bible and comfort in God. Read the Gospels beginning with the Book of John."

"Are you a pastor?" she asked.

"No, just an ordinary Christian," he answered as he humbly walked to his car.

Proverbs 17:22 helps us grasp the ups and downs of life this way: **"A joyful heart is good medicine, but a broken spirit dries the** bones." Barry and I are savvy enough to know that life events can hit people really hard. Not everyone walking around with a "sunny side up Smiley Face" feels that way in their heart. Broken hearts are easy to conceal, and broken spirits can turn people into mere skeletons of themselves.

But a well-timed, appropriate response to cover a person standing there exposed can become a turning point of hope. This isn't about the cultural chic of random acts of kindness. This is about being candid with people dealing with life-threatening news by telling them that God is greater than their worst fears.

In the Book of Numbers, the Lord spoke to Moses telling him to have Aaron the High Priest bless the people with this blessing: **"The Lord bless you and keep you; the Lord make His face to shine upon you and be gracious to you; the Lord lift up His countenance on you and give you peace." (Numbers 6:22-26)** The Living Bible says it this way, **"May the Lord's face radiate with joy because of you." (vs 26)** Our "sunny side up eggs in the frying pan" picture characterize God's face that radiates with joy over you, no matter what. That means that God smiles when you can't, God keeps you when you give up, He gives you peace when you are torn and His face shines brightly enough to illuminate your darkest times.

YOUR THOUGHTS

LIGHTEN UP!

READ NUMBERS 32:20-25

C ruising through my neighborhood on the way to the store, life seemed so sublime until I spotted a hand-painted yard sign with black letters that read: **"Your sin will find you out! Numbers 32:23"** Whoa! I heard the celestial hammer come down with a thud. I thought I was on a road trip not a guilt trip! Jarring, harsh and full of condemnation, the message "God is mad at you!" came across from those saints who forgot that they were once sinners, too.

After shopping, I went home and looked up the Bible reference they cited. Surprisingly, I found that this warning did not pertain to passing motorists. In the Old Testament, Moses warned the tribes of Gad and Reuben not to settle into their new land without first helping their brothers to conquer the Promised Land. In context, God was warning His people not to sin by becoming complacent, settling down in their own land and not caring about their brothers.

On that same busy street where the excoriating sign is displayed is a Walmart that is always packed with people. Some people loathe to shop at Walmart, but I don't mind because I always find bargains there. This trip, I scooped up some store-manager specials and enjoyed some deep-pocket savings.

I stepped into the check-out lane and a young Asian man rang up my order, taking extra time to bag my items carefully. Behind my order on the conveyor belt was a gallon of milk, a package of Oreo cookies and a package of Chips Ahoy cookies— all my favorites!

I glanced at the couple behind me who decided to take their chances at Walmart for the sake of milk and cookies. The woman was mid-seventies, heavy-set and wearing old, mismatched separates. The husband looked a little rough, unshaven with long stringy gray hair.

I made a quick mental estimation of them. *"These people are just trying to take a break from whatever they are going through by coming out to buy their favorite comfort foods,"* I thought.

I turned to the sweet Asian cashier, pointed to the milk and cookies, and said, "Please ring these items up on my bill and bag them separately." The couple behind me looked shocked and thanked me several times.

"Please go have a party!" I said, as I smiled and paid for their order. There you have it! Don't be complacent in loving others. Do

something to lighten someone's heavy load. Lift their heart with some sudden kindness and help them find God, not run away from Him.

People may go to Walmart for more reasons than just shopping. Maybe the store seems like an oasis for tired, lonely people or it feels festive and luxurious with all its products and activity. Or maybe they can get their junk food cheaper there, I don't know.

Here is the underlying spiritual dynamic that we need to understand. When people discover God's goodness and intimate love for them, they don't want to sin anymore. They want to clean up their lives to please God because He is so wonderful to know.

Looking up the word "find" during my research, I found many great reasons to respond to God: Proverbs 3:4 says you will find favor and a good reputation. Matthew 11:29 says you will find rest for your soul. Hebrews 4:16 says you will find mercy and grace. And Matthew 16:25 says you will find eternal life. All these reasons and more should convince us to offer God's love and goodness to people we meet at every juncture. We need to lighten up and light the way for others to find Jesus, our Comforter and Friend.

YOUR THOUGHTS

THE THINGS MONEY CAN'T BUY

READ 1 TIMOTHY 6:6-11

*T*he $2 bill has a long history in America dating back to 1862 when it was first printed and circulated. Obscure as it is now, back then it was a hefty sum of money. The bill bearing the portrait of Thomas Jefferson was discontinued in 1966. To celebrate America's Bicentennial, the U.S. Treasury brought the bills back into print in 1976.

Most people who have $2 bills nowadays don't spend them. Instead, they store them away, saving them as collector's items, in hopes they will someday increase in value. Except for some extremely old, rare mints though, the current value remains at $2.

Currency is typically regarded as a means of purchasing goods and services using government issued banknotes or coins. In everyday society, money is a means of obtaining things that we need to live. People determine their own appetites for what they think they need and what they are willing to do to acquire money. The scramble to obtain money can induce people to easily cross moral lines into immoral or illegal means depending on their personal desire for "more."

The Apostle Paul cites this propensity to break the rules for the cause of money this way. **"And if we have food and covering, with these we shall be content. But those who want to get rich fall into temptation and a snare and many foolish and harmful desires which plunge men into ruin and destruction. For the love of money is a root of all sorts of evil, and some by longing for it have wandered away from the faith and pierced themselves with many a pang." (1 Timothy 6:8-10)**

Money itself is not an evil thing. The way our society operates, money is a necessity. The love of money is the vision or aura of money in which we picture wealth enhancing us. This is the imaginary picture that can drive us. In our minds, if money is everything, then we mentally crown it "king." The scripture warns that the dark side of this singular focus can plunge us to the depths of financial ruin and self-destruction.

There is another wrong view of money that, in our piety, is also wrong. The view that money is nothing, that those who pursue it are materialistic and we are spiritually better than them implies that personal poverty is noble or even godly. Unfortunately, our wrong view cuts us off from using our worldly success to help others, the true definition of godliness.

This wrong view enables people to adopt lazy nonchalance to support themselves. Refusing to work in the workplace is not a way to trust God to supply our needs. In fact, it spurns that faith. The Bible strongly condemns laziness and refusal to work. **"If anyone will not work, neither let him eat. For we hear that some among you are leading an undisciplined life, doing no work at all, but acting like busybodies." (2 Thessalonians 3:10-11)**

Both mindsets, "money is everything" and "money is nothing" are extremes to be avoided because they are not the way that leads to true happiness, peace, and contentment. Money does not soothe our soul. It does not quiet our heart from the daily noise and din. Nor does it halt our anxieties or solve our problems. On the other hand, idleness makes us unproductive and immature. Instead, we need Christ to come and relieve our burdens from our worldly existence.

Hear the words of Christ Jesus who beckons us to come to Him and enjoy rest in His arms. **"Come to Me, all you who are weary and heavy-laden, and I will give you rest. Take My yoke upon you, and learn from Me, for I am gentle and humble in heart; and you shall find rest for your souls. For My yoke is easy, and my burden is light." (Matthew 11:28-30)** He promises to release us from the pressure and worries of life that can consume us. Whether our cares are due to the abundance of money or the lack of it, Jesus opens His arms to take our stress upon Himself. We can trust Him to work things out and bring us through difficult times. Rest for our souls is not just wishful thinking. This is a true reality that can be ours. The value of Christ's power and compassion is something that currency, no matter what denomination, cannot buy.

YOUR THOUGHTS

ARE YOU LONELY AND BLUE?

READ 2 CORINTHIANS 1:3-7

B lue Jays are intensely beautiful birds that can be spotted in North American and Canada. They are related to crows and can mimic the calls of other birds. Most interestingly, they are not lonely. They keep the same mate throughout their lifetime and have an extensive social system, living within family groups. Sometimes their children join the group, adding to the mix of one big happy family. They may be blue, but they are not lonely!

How about you? Does loneliness make you feel blue lately? Staying home alone during Covid, long hard winters, or other life events that isolate us can make us sad and give us a case of the blues.

Loneliness is a malaise distinct from just being alone. Loneliness can take our mind, will and emotions captive, blanketing our being with a deep sadness or even despair.

Situations that we can't control may contribute to our sense of separation. In the workplace, working long hours or odd hours can remove us from social involvement. Long-term illness or recovery from an operation can affect our well-being, not to mention dealing with physical pain or the fear of the unknown. Aging can certainly bring on loneliness as, one-by-one, we see our friends and family members dying. Other causes of loneliness are divorce, unemployment, or death of a spouse, all sending the emotions spiraling downward. Is there anything we can do to escape the blues?

I will mention a couple of things that are available to us that don't really work to reach us in our emotions. These are just temporary Band-Aids. Watching endless hours of television just to see other people and have their voices in the room may seem very helpful. Unfortunately, this fix will only numb you as you affix yourself to your recliner.

Social media and online games may entertain us for a while, but again the real medicine is found in human contact not in monotonous game playing. Be careful not to be drawn into cult-like websites that prey on the needs of lonely people. Do not risk safety or savings by believing bad actors who present themselves online.

Let's turn to the promise of God's ability to comfort and care for us. Psalm 68:5-6 explains who God is for us. **"A Father of the fatherless and a judge for the widows, is God in his holy habitation. God**

makes a home for the lonely; He leads out the prisoners into prosperity..."

God may seem austere as we picture Him here in His holy temple, unaffected by human suffering. This passage corrects that view by saying that, although He is up there, He is also down here in our midst. He is far but also very near, actively paying close attention to the needs of the lonely and the afflicted. He may be removed, but He is not aloof. This dual proximity of our holy God is the celebration of the Psalmist. Orphans, widows, and prisoners all have access to Him in their dire need. This gives us hope that God is accessible and responsive to us also.

Another passage is a similar celebration of God's willingness to meet us in 2 Corinthians 1:3-4. **"Blessed be the God and Father of our Lord Jesus Christ, the Father of mercies and God of all comfort who comforts us in all our affliction..."** Again, God encompasses the title of the Supreme Father who watches over His children, caring for them.

The word "comfort" in the Old Testament language means "to wrap" as in binding up a wound. Let's face it, loneliness is an emotional wound like having a hole in your heart. We feel empty, unloved, and forsaken.

In the New Testament Greek, it means "solace" which is a resolve or relief from our despondency. God has a way of responding to our loneliness by filling our heart with His love for us. Never underestimate the reach of the Holy Spirit to keep us out of despair.

Here are some practical steps to combat loneliness and escape the blues. First, take consolation in who God is for you. Re-read these two scripture verses and take them to heart. Tell God that you need Him, and you need others. Be open about your feelings and don't downplay your emotions.

Second, ask God for new opportunities to make friends and join new groups. Step out in faith as He opens doors for you. Come out of your lonely prison cell and make plans to meet new people.

Third, make new friends by being a good friend. Don't make relationships all about yourself. Learn how to care about others. Be a good listener. There may be someone you can help along the way.

Finally, don't just wait for people to contact you. Reach out to people in your sphere. Get in touch with longtime friends. Make lunch or dinner dates. Step out of your comfort zone. Solve your social vacuum by joining a group, a church, a gym, or volunteer organization. Start participating in activities to meet new people. God will open doors that are suitable for you. Be encouraged and look forward. Worship and praise God for who He is, and you won't be blue anymore!

THE VALUE OF GOAL SETTING

READ PHILIPPIANS 3:10-14

I don't believe in making New Year's Resolutions because they usually never materialize. Instead, I adhere to setting goals to achieve a future desired outcome to benefit my family and me. Holding yourself to daily, weekly, monthly, and yearly goals give you a doable framework to accomplish your dreams. Planning is key to self-discipline and self-development. Executing that plan launches you forward as you take on your goals in measured amounts.

Although it is very practical, there is nothing unspiritual about goal setting. Faith always looks forward and belief rigorously trusts God for all things. The Bible says, **"The mind of man plans his way, but** the Lord directs his steps." (Proverbs 16:9) Your actions give God something to work with as He orchestrates the outcome for you.

The outlook of fatalism comes when a person has no goals, no hopes, and no expectations for the future. It is a life of resignation that nothing will ever get better. With that pessimism, the days will seem mundane and futile. You merely exist because life lacks purpose and meaning. In your head, you live life facing backwards, reminiscing about the past that you cannot undo. You might give up and stop caring about anything.

To stay out of the numbness of fatalism, ask God to reveal His purposes for you. His goals for you are life-giving and worthwhile. Philippians 1:6 reminds us that God began a good work when we were born. **"He who began a good work in you will perfect it until the day of Christ Jesus."** You simply need to discover what that good work is.

Philippians 1:25 mentions the word "progress." This means that God wants you to improve with the skills that He has given you to learn, grow, and excel. Your growth and progress glorify Him. Philippians 2:13 says, **"For it is God who is at work in you, both to will and to work for His good pleasure."** God works within you to accomplish the good works for which He created you. If you let Him, this partnership with Jesus can be exhilarating. These activities are reasonable, beneficial, and satisfying when we learn to plan and set goals for ourselves.

Be careful to stay out of fuzzy, unrealistic, fantasy-filled ideas that you invent in your imagination. Don't decide what you think God should do for you. That is irreverent and backwards as you shout orders and expect Him to obey. Instead, humbly seek God for His goals for you. He will reveal specific, measurable, achievable, realistic opportunities to you. Most likely, they will involve helping other people, serving in your community, or spreading the Good News of Jesus to others.

Finally, Philippians 3:13-14 ascribes to a life facing forward motivated by future events. "**...But one thing I do; forgetting what lies behind and reaching forward to what lies ahead, I press on toward the goal for the prize of the upward call of God in Christ Jesus.**" Past experiences lay behind us from which we draw knowledge. Today is when we plan for tomorrow. Our vision for attainment and accomplishment keeps us moving forward towards our future. Let God give you dreams and goals that you will enjoy. As a result, your life will be full and satisfying knowing that you are working toward achievements that really matter.

YOUR THOUGHTS

OVERCOMING PROCRASTINATION

READ JAMES 4:6-17

I pride myself on keeping a clean house. Without notice, someone could stop by and tour my home without stepping over piles of dirty clothes or a week's worth of garbage. No negative judgments would I endure from an impromptu guest, shocked at what they see. Dishes are washed, laundry is done, and my house is mess-free... except for my basement workbench. That is my eyesore, the one disorganized pile I haven't touched. It keeps getting worse because I use it as my catch-all landing place for junk, hidden away downstairs like a dirty secret!

Why? Because I am guilty of the habit of procrastination. This is the mind-game that we play, telling ourselves that we can put off doing something until "later." It is like a clock that has three hands. The big hand is for the hour, the little hand is for the minutes, and a third hand is marked "later." Unfortunately, the habitual delay of projects only compounds the work we need to do. If we cave to the lulling promise of "later," then projects stockpile, bills and paperwork accumulate, and tasks seem insurmountable. Eventually, we find ourselves overwhelmed and become discouraged.

Overcoming chronic procrastination requires identifying its appeal, admitting our lack of urgency, and adopting a "now" mentality. We can free ourselves from those guilty feelings when we get busy and do something that needs to be done. We will feel empowered from a sense of accomplishment that propels us forward.

Let's see what the Bible says about procrastination. **"Therefore, to one who knows the right thing to do, and does not do it, to him it is sin." (James 4:17)** This says that we know what we are supposed to do, but for some reason, we don't or won't do it. Fear, apathy, disinterest, or downright laziness block our way. Rather than face our weak-willed habit, we tell ourselves, "I'll do it later," and push the timeline to some undetermined future. Not doing our dirty laundry is one thing, but ignoring the promptings of the Holy Spirit to act for God is much more serious. The Bible says that inaction is as much of a sin as wrong action.

Don't put off the opportunities that God lays ahead for you. Now is the call to action! Muster self-discipline to identify fear, laziness, and guilt. Desire motivation by giving yourself good reasons to act. The fix is found in this scripture: **"For God does not give us** a spirit of timidity (fear), but a spirit of power, of love and of self-discipline." (2 Timothy 1:7) God says that He will give us the power to overcome procrastination. He will help us move on our practical projects and spiritual callings. We can acquire the discipline to carry out the things on our "to do" list. He gives us the power to move forward with our practical projects, such as finishing that remodeling job. And the self-discipline to carry out the things that we know we need to do, such as reading the Bible every day. God will give us the ability to exert power in the little things and in the vital things.

By His Spirit, we can have a clear, organized mind to accomplish our tasks and personal goals. A sense of victory will energize us. We will gain a sense of pride and self-honor when we see ourselves becoming proactive. Heading off problems before they snowball will save us time, money, and peace of mind in the long run. That is love, power, and self-discipline in motion.

Like my workbench, let's take it piece by piece, put everything in its place and eventually clean it up. Let's stop making excuses and learn to live higher by believing in God's power to accomplish what we know we need to do.

YOUR THOUGHTS

CHILDLIKENESS IS CHRISTLIKENESS

READ MATTHEW 18:1-6

*O*ne night I stayed up late reading, leaning comfortably against the couch armrest under the glow of a floor lamp. I was engrossed in a tense story about a kidnapping. I was finally getting to the good part about how the victim safely escapes when my husband came downstairs to check on me.

"Are you still up?" he asked, his voice registering low because he was tired. I wasn't expecting a man's deep voice calling me from the darkness. It startled me like the surprise scene in a scary movie. Instinctively, I threw the book as my arms and legs fluttered back and forth, like a beetle landing on its back frantically trying to right itself!

"You scared me!" I yelped. He didn't mean to frighten me, but my reaction was comical.

"You must have jumped a foot off the couch!" he quipped as he came towards me.

"I just finished the creepy part of this book and that was still in my mind," I said in my defense.

He started laughing about my reaction so much that he laid down on the living room floor, rolling with laughter until he cried. I had never seen him laugh so hard!

I feigned being upset with him, although I wasn't. That gave my prankster husband the added drama he craved. Watching him roll around helplessly laughing as he recounted the scene made me smile. Here was my 70-year-old hubby on the floor in his pajamas losing it like someone was tickling him! He was like a little kid finding humor at my expense, so I let him have his moment.

That same kind of innocent behavior was what Jesus referred to when He brought a nearby child to Himself to give the Disciples a lesson on humility. The account in the Gospel of Mark notes that the Disciples had been arguing among themselves about who would be the greatest in the coming Kingdom. The Gospel of Matthew picks up from their question to Jesus.

"At that time the disciples came to Jesus saying, 'Who then is the greatest in the kingdom of heaven?' And He called a child to

Himself and set him before them, and said, 'Truly I say to you, unless you are converted and become like children, you shall not enter the kingdom of heaven. Whoever then humbles himself as this child, he is the greatest in the kingdom of heaven.'" (Matthew 18:1-4)

The question for us now is, "How do you become like a child when you are an adult? What does God expect from us as grown-ups?" Let's first address the Disciples' attitude of high-mindedness and vision of self-importance. The Book of Romans explains what Jesus was getting at. **"Be of the same mind towards one another; do not be haughty in mind...Do not be wise in your own estimation."** **(Romans 12:16)** The first step towards humility is to get rid of the picture of yourself as being better than others.

God expects us to reorient ourselves by reversing our superior mindsets. We must humble ourselves in our own estimation and recalibrate our view of others. Have respect for other people rather than contempt. Filter your impulses before you act upon them by pulling back from caustic, haughty remarks.

Jesus said to be innocent like a child who has never had malicious thoughts. A child naturally has love and trust in his heart. Innocence is pure, untainted, and guileless. God can show us how to be pure in heart if we ask Him. **"Blessed are the pure in heart for they will see God." (Matthew 5:8)** Humility is the beginning of greatness attainable by all. Love and trust God, and love others by wanting the best for them.

Learn to find simple, uncomplicated pleasures in life. Enjoy having fun, clowning around, and making others laugh. Even more, teach yourself to lighten up, be silly, let go and have a good belly laugh on the floor in your pajamas whenever you can because childlikeness is Christlikeness.

YOUR THOUGHTS

THE FRUIT OF THE VINE

READ JOHN 2:1-12

C heers! This is the hallmark of the holidays; the quintessential salutation followed by the clink of wine glasses raised in unison. The crystal stemware held up against the festive room lights reflect tiny rainbows caught within the patterns of the cut glass. People voice their genuine well-wishes to extend hopes for health and prosperity to others, and partygoers sip their favorite vintage to culminate the toast.

Wine-drinking, toasts, and merriment are conventional features of grand occasions such as weddings or private settings among family and friends. The fruit of the vine adds a timeless cultural ambiance that speaks of enjoyment, relationships, and hospitality.

Such was the case at a wedding in Cana of Galilee according to the Book of John Chapter 2. Jesus, His mother, Mary, and the Disciples were among the welcomed guests in attendance. The festivities were in full swing until Mary noticed that all the wine was gone. She turned to Jesus and told Him to intervene. **"They have no wine,"** she said. **(John 2:3)**

Notably, this event was the beginning of Jesus' public ministry. A crucial pivot took place when Jesus rebuked her by saying, **"Woman, what do I have to do with you?" (vs 4)** Then He referred to His eventual crucifixion. **"My hour has not yet come." (vs 4)** A bewildered Mary submitted to the chastisement and accepted the lordship that He asserted. She told the surrounding servants, **"Whatever He says to you, do it." (vs 5)**

Jesus was now free from human parental constraints. He saw the stone waterpots in the home used for Jewish purification rites and told the servants to fill them with water. He directed them to draw some of the water out and take it to the headwaiter. By the time the water was carried to the head table, it miraculously turned into wine.

Without knowing where the wine came from, the headwaiter gave the bridegroom a compliment on his remarkable hospitality. **"Every man serves the good wine first, and when men have drunk freely, then that which is poorer; you have kept the good wine until now." (vs 10)** In other words, most hosts serve the inferior wine after guests are feeling good from the better wine and don't care. But this host saved the best wine for the latter part of the gala.

Bible commentary sets forth that the better wine served at the end of the wedding feast signified the New Covenant that Jesus came to establish. As a result of this first miracle, the Disciples believed in Jesus as God's power was manifested. This is all wonderful, but I believe there is much more to this scene, especially if you ask the question, "Why was this first miracle so discreet?"

For the rest of His ministry recorded in the Book of John, Jesus referred to Himself as the sole emissary of heaven acting upon the explicit will of God the Father. **"Jesus said to them, 'My food is to do the will of Him who sent Me and to accomplish His work.'"** (John 4:34) This meant that there was nothing random about the ministry of Jesus. His actions were deliberate and precise, perfectly ordered by God the Father and empowered by God the Spirit. The life and ministry of Jesus was all about heavenly disclosure—revealing God to man. **"He who has seen Me has seen the Father."** (John 14:9) At long last, the invisible unseen God could be seen and known in Jesus.

Now let's look back with a wider lens at the wedding of Cana. Jesus was a key guest who used His supernatural power to make sure that the wedding feast was a success. This was where His ministry began, but it continues in the Book of Revelation where He is described as the Bridegroom who is glorified beyond all measure! **"Let us rejoice and be glad and give the glory to Him, for the marriage of the Lamb has come and His bride has made herself ready."** **(Revelation 19:7)**

God the Father used the wedding at Cana to show us a picture of the ultimate wedding feast where Jesus is married to His people, and they are forever united. He saved the best wine for last. The New

Covenant of grace through faith enables us to enjoy His gripping presence, love, joy, peace, and security now and forever. The first miracle proves the incredible miracle of God's saving power, as celebrated by the multitudes at the marriage supper of the Lamb. **"Bless are those who are invited to the marriage supper of the Lamb." (Revelation 19:9)** The wedding at Cana was a picture of the celebration of all celebrations in heaven, and the reason for our hope and joy now.

The words of the Apostle Paul ring out with the cadence of a toast as he looks ahead to this same glorious scene. **"I pray that the eyes of your heart may be enlightened, so that you may know what is the hope of His calling, what are the riches of the glory of His inheritance in the saints and what is the surpassing greatness of His power toward us who believe." (Ephesians 1:18)** To this I raise my glass along with well-wishes and say, "Cheers!"

LOST AND FOUND

READ JOHN 10:1-15

O ur cat, Striper, routinely stands on the back of our living room couch, parts the curtains with his nose and looks out the window, scanning the front yard for birds, squirrels or anything that moves. My neighbors have seen him do this and have commented on how adorable he is.

One morning as I backed out of the driveway on my way to work, I noticed him watching me from the front window. Seeing him there touched me, so I waved a cheesy "good-bye" from inside the car. I was embarrassed when a driver of a car who came up fast in my rear-view mirror saw me do this. I'm sure he was not as sentimental about my "cat mom waves and blows kisses" moment as I was!

Oh well! This just shows that pets are vital members of our families. The endearment goes even deeper when the pet is a rescue. When animals are rescued from potential harm, it seems like they never forget and become attached to their rescuers for the rest of their lives.

Such is the case with Striper. He is a healthy indoor cat with a full run of the house. He curls up on the bed and sleeps all day, prowls at night, nibbles plenty of good food, slurps fresh water from his bowl and enjoys a clean litterbox. He leads an enviable cat life today, but it almost didn't go this well for him. I am going to tell his story of how I found him, even though it is unsettling to read. Keep in mind that this is the context for our parable of Jesus as the Good Shepherd.

Several years ago, in early January the temperature in Cleveland, Ohio was 60 degrees. I took advantage of the spring-like weather by going for a walk on my favorite fitness trail at a nearby park. I briskly walked the first stretch and was turning the bend when I heard a woman calling me.

"Lady! Lady!" she called out. "Do you know where I can take a stray cat? I found him in a bag inside a garbage can!"

"What?" I thought. *"Who would dump a live cat into a park garbage can?"* I spun around and saw a young woman and her mother walking towards me. She showed me the insulated food bag that she found the cat in. She heard him crying while they were walking, and she pulled him out.

Still shocked, I told her that there was a pet shelter near the park entrance. She could take him there since it would likely be open. I guessed that they might charge a fee to drop off unwanted pets.

"I have him in the back seat of my car," she said. "Do you want to see him before I take him there?"

"Sure!" I shrugged. "I love cats."

She opened the back door of her car. Curled up on the back seat was a frightened brown-striped, short-hair tabby. He had gorgeous green eyes and striped symmetrical markings. I scooped him up and held him. He seemed to relax in my arms as I fell in love with him.

I will take him home with me," I told her. "If he doesn't get along with my older female cat then I will take him to the pet shelter."

She seemed relieved, thanked me, and drove off. I walked back to my car holding my newfound kitten. On the way home I named him "Striper."

"Don't worry Striper," I assured him. "You are safe with me now."

That happened about five years ago. Since then, my older female cat passed away, leaving Striper as king of the house. He is well-adjusted, social, and super-friendly with visitors. The happy ending is that he gets to live out his feline existence thanks to a well-timed rescue.

Now let's use this story for the analogy of Jesus the Good Shepherd who rescues lost sheep. In Matthew 18:11 Jesus begins the parable of the lost sheep by saying, **"For the Son of Man has come to save that which is lost."** Here, Jesus positions Himself as the ultimate Rescuer of people.

Luke 15:4 Jesus tells this same parable to the Pharisees in response to their complaints about Him socializing with "sinners." The lost sheep in the story represent people who are separated from God by their sin. He reasons with the Pharisees, saying that any decent man who owns a flock of 100 sheep would leave 99 of them to go out and recover the one sheep that lost its way. When he finds it, he carries it safely home, and all the friends and neighbors rejoice that the sheep was found. Unlike the resentful Pharisees, Jesus says all the angels in heaven rejoice over one sinner who renounces his sin and turns to God.

John 10:1-15 Jesus again uses the comparison of people to lost sheep. **"The sheep hear his voice, and he calls his own sheep by name, and leads them out." (John 10:4)** Jesus warns of the dangers of falling prey to wolves and thieves when we are away from God. The crowd that was listening to Him did not understand what He meant. He told them directly that they were the lost sheep in the story. They needed Him as their Rescuer.

As unsettling as it is to hear about lost animals, it is way more disconcerting to picture yourself as being lost, alone, helpless, and vulnerable to the elements of the world. That is exactly where Jesus was going with this parable. He wanted people to realize their lost condition in their sin and their dire need of a Savior. He singled out the one lost sheep because we each need a personal rescue from sin. Jesus saves us on an individual basis because He is a personal Savior.

Jesus cushions this difficult imagery by saying that He can be trusted as the Good Shepherd, much like I assured Striper that he was safe with me. Jesus supernaturally brings us to Himself and carries us to safe pasture. He is the resting place for our hearts. In Him, we find love, acceptance, safety, and eternal security.

Jesus is the good and trustworthy Shepherd because He laid down His life for His sheep. **"I am the good shepherd; the good shepherd lays down his life for the sheep." (John 10:11)** By dying on the Cross, Jesus paid the penalty of sin once and for all. When we personally accept His sacrifice on our behalf, we can be forgiven and released from sin's penalty of death. Christ makes sure that people understand the cost to Him. No one else can pay such a high price to redeem us. Jesus is the only Good Shepherd who was sent from God for this purpose.

For us now, His rescue is simply a prayer away. His forgiveness of sin is free for the asking. Then we will be forever grateful and amazed, just like the hymn "Amazing Grace:" says: "Amazing grace, how sweet the sound, that saved a wretch like me. I once was lost but now I'm found; was blind but now I see." And we will be forever indebted to our Rescuer who is Jesus.

YOUR THOUGHTS

SCOREBOARD

READ TITUS 3:1-7

We live near a community football stadium where local high school teams compete for conference titles and state championships. Sports fans park their cars at a nearby shopping mall and walk to the stadium carrying their padded cushions, binoculars, blankets and thermoses of hot coffee. From our window we can detect the distant glow of the field lights illuminating the night games and we can hear the rousing cheers when a team scores.

As the teams huddle to plan their next play, all eyes are on the black and white scoreboard that is fixed at one end of the field. The scoreboard dutifully keeps count of every point earned and displays the final score to the entire neighborhood. That scoreboard always has the last say, announcing the fate of the team branded either "winner" or "loser."

I have friends who are avid football fans. They remember the scores of the games played by their favorite teams, who they played, when and by how much they either won or lost. It is like they carry a scoreboard in their mind that helps them keep track of every season.

Football trivia is fascinating for those who have the memory capacity to keep it all straight. Players, stats, fumbles, touchdowns, and surprising victories are compartmentalized in a cerebral filing cabinet, ready to pull out and share with fellow football addicts!

The ability to remember is a blessing from God. That ability is part of the power of living that He gives all of us. "...**though He is not far from each of us; for in Him we live and move and exist."** **(Acts 17:28)** Some versions of the Bible say, "have our being." Due to basic cognitive abilities, we can usually recall people's names when we see them, remember faces, occasions, milestones such as graduations, first car and first jobs. First loves are especially embedded within us along with the heartbreak of relationships that did not work out.

Among all the good experiences that we live through, there are also difficulties we wished had never happened. Some of those events were life-altering and consequential. People also experience deep personal offenses that, no doubt, cause lasting pain.

Our natural reaction to emotionally handle those types of offenses is to inwardly erect a "scoreboard" to keep track of offenses. We rehearse them in our mind and then vividly describe them to other people. We may carry the outrage in us for many years, keeping the memory alive. At some point, though, we would do well to apply forgiveness to those deep wounds.

By offering this lesson on forgiveness, I am in no way diminishing the hurtful situations that people have been through. I am sure these events were very hard to go through. I wish we had a better world to live in, where people value the lives of their fellow human beings. Unfortunately for right now, we don't.

"For we also once were foolish ourselves, disobedient, deceived, enslaved to various lusts and pleasures, spending our life in malice and envy, hateful, hating one another." (Titus 3:3) The problem comes when, as this scripture cites, we spend our life in the trap of hating others for the harm they caused us. We never move on from those memories and they start to haunt us in an all-consuming way. The offenses we have stored are all we think about and all we talk about. They are a cancer to our soul, eating us up inside. Erecting that "scoreboard" and then continually adding to it makes us live our life recounting offenses and wallowing in history that cannot be changed.

The way to break free from this habit is to realize that, although we possess the power to live, we also need power beyond our scope to forgive and forget. We need God's power to find emotional healing for offenses that have piled up over the years.

The scripture continues, **"But when the kindness of God our Savior and His love for mankind appeared, He saved us, not on the basis of deeds, which we have done in righteousness, but according to mercy, by the washing of regeneration and**

renewing by the Holy Spirit." (Titus 3:4-5) God loves mankind and has the power to reach us deep inside where our pain is stored. He can renew those parts of us that have been damaged so badly. He can wash those soul wounds clean.

First, we need to seek God and ask for His forgiveness of our offenses. **"Forgive us our debts as we also have forgiven our debtors."** (Matthew 6:12) By turning to Christ and asking for His help, He can effectively erase our "scoreboard" and wipe out the calculations. We will still remember the incidents, but the pain will be removed, and sin will no longer have power over us.

Ask Jesus to come to your aid and help you to forgive. He will enable you to have the healing that you need. As you recall the incidents and the perpetrators involved, mention them to God and ask Him to renew you. We can absolutely experience the cleansing of our conscience. **"If we confess our sins, He is faithful and righteous to forgive us our sins and to cleanse us from all unrighteousness."** (1 John 1:9)

We read in 2 Corinthians 13:5 that love keeps no record of wrongs. **"Love...does not take into account a wrong suffered..."** When we choose to love rather than hate our offenders, we take our life back from them and look forward instead of backwards. We can move on and live in creative ways rather than be haunted by our memories.

We can form a new habit to replace the "scoreboard" by leaning into God's love each time we feel offended. God's love is infinitely greater than all the harm we have experienced. It is a matter of choosing to let go of our past and trusting God for His love that covers a multitude of sins.

YOUR THOUGHTS

THE DAY ELVIS DIED

READ HEBREWS 4:14-16

I remember the day Elvis Presley died; August 17, 1977. I was working at a bridal salon inside a shopping mall in Florence, Kentucky. When the news of his death broke, our store manager, who was a devoted Elvis fan, began crying uncontrollably. She had to leave work early because she was so distraught.

The rest of us at the store were saddened by the news, but it didn't affect us like it did her. We were not in love with Elvis as much as she obviously was. During his career, his fans dubbed him "King." He held that sacred place in the hearts of millions and, for some of them, the world stopped that day.

Fast forward, on Thursday January 12, 2023, Lisa Marie Presley, the only daughter of Elvis and Pricilla Presley, died of cardiac arrest. She was only 54 years old. Five months prior to her death, she published an essay in *People Magazine*, baring her soul about the haunting grief she suffered from her son's suicide death at age 27.

In her essay she wrote, "Death is part of life whether we like it or not— and so is grieving. Grief does not stop or go away, a year or so after the loss. Grief is something you will have to carry with you for the rest of your life...You do not 'get over it,' you do not 'move on,' period...Nothing, absolutely NOTHING takes away the pain but finding support can help you feel a little bit less alone." [3]

Losing a child from suicide or any other cause is probably the most devastating tragedy a doting parent can experience. In her article, Lisa Marie said she beat herself up daily, blaming herself for her son's death. No doubt it took a horrible toll on her conscience.

Any death of a loved one is painfully hard, leaving an indelible mark on us. I was close to my mother and was her primary caregiver when she was older. After she died, I felt like I lost my right arm. There was an unmistakable void that could never again be filled.

As Lisa Marie noted, emptiness and loneliness set in whenever someone close to us dies. We are used to having that parent, child, spouse, sibling, or best friend. We hear their voice, feel them, do things with them and for them; then suddenly they are gone. Permanency is the sting of death that is soul-shattering. There is no reversal, no going back, just stone-cold silence on the other side.

---

3. People Magazine, January 30, 2023

Our lot is that death is relentlessly cruel. Facing this, the question for the survivor becomes; Will you allow grief to cripple you? Will you let your heartache stop you from living and take you to an early grave as in Lisa Marie's case?

To answer that, I want to gently insert another question. Is it true that, as Lisa Marie wrote, "Nothing, absolutely NOTHING" will ever take away the pain? I can say with certainty that there is help for our troubled hearts beyond human kindness and support. Let's find out where that help begins.

John Chapter 11 begins with the dire sickness of Lazarus, the dear brother of Martha and Mary of Bethany. These siblings were known to host Jesus and His Disciples when they were in town. Jesus grew so close to them that He was like a family member. The sisters sent word to Jesus that Lazarus was sick, counting on Him to come heal their brother.

Instead, Jesus delayed His trip two days until He knew that Lazarus was dead. This seemed odd to the Disciples. Jesus knew, however, that this illness was designated to reveal the glory of God. He said to the wondering Disciples, **"Our friend Lazarus has fallen asleep; but I go, that I may awaken him out of sleep." (John 11:11)** Then Jesus clarified His term "sleep." **"Lazarus is dead...but let us go to him."** He told them plainly. **(John 11: 14-15)**

When they arrived in Bethany, Martha ran to meet Jesus saying that if He had come sooner, her brother would not have died. Her sister Mary was so grieved that she did not leave the house. Jesus responded to Martha: **"Your brother shall rise again." (John 11:23)** Martha agreed about the bodily resurrection of all who believe someday.

Jesus countered her again. Yes, someday, and also now. **"Jesus said to her, 'I am the resurrection and the life; he who believes in Me shall live even if he dies, and everyone who lives and believes in Me shall never die. Do you believe this?"** (John 11: 25-26) Yes, she said, she believed.

Jesus went to the home of Martha and Mary. He saw the grieving household along with Jewish friends of the family. People all around Him were stricken from the loss of a brother, a favorite host and friend, crying inconsolably. Jesus was deeply moved and wept alongside them.

Although Jesus knew the outcome of this purposeful death, He was not unsympathetic to the mourners. Sifting through a myriad of emotions, Jesus used the moment to steel Himself against man's paramount enemy—Death.

Composing Himself, He asked them, **"Where have you laid him?"** **(John 11: 34)** They led Him to a cave with a stone covering the entrance. They protested that there would be an awful stench since Lazarus had been dead for four days. Jesus insisted, **"Did I not say to you, if you believe you will see the glory of God?"** (vs 35) They obeyed Him and removed the stone. Jesus cried out in a loud voice for everyone in the crowd to hear, **"Lazarus, come forth!"** (vs 36) In an incredible frightening moment, the dead brother appeared and walked out of the cave wrapped in his grave cloths.

"Unbind him and let him go." **(John 11:44)** He said. The news of the miraculous resurrection of Lazarus traveled throughout the area. Some people believed when they heard, and others did not. Regardless, Jesus used this death and bodily resurrection for

God's glory, pointing to Himself as the sole Conqueror of Death, The Resurrection and the Life.

Going back to our question if NOTHING removes the pain of death, this scene proves that the risen Christ can cradle our hearts if we let Him. John 11:26 assures us, **"and everyone who lives and believes in Me shall not die."** His message was for the living. God will not allow our hearts to die alongside our dear departed one. The memory of the death will always remain, but not the debilitating pain, guilt and heartache. This may seem impossible, but that is what the miracle in John 11 qualified Jesus to do. Now the question is; Do *you* believe this?

The writer of Hebrews celebrates Jesus as our High Priest, established by God to act as our intermediary to dispense help and healing to people. **"Since then we have a great high priest who has passed through the heavens, Jesus the Son of God, let us hold fast to our confession. For we do not have a high priest who cannot sympathize with our weaknesses...Let us therefore draw near with confidence to the throne of grace, that we may receive mercy and find grace to help in time of need." (Hebrews 4:14-16)**

During our darkest times of profound grief, we need to look up and see Jesus, who is willing to comfort and console us. We do not have to go through those times alone. He will inhabit our emptiness and loneliness with His presence and peace. Then, in an inexplicable way, we will stand up against Death and say resolutely, **"O Death, where is your victory? O Death, where is your sting?" (1 Corinthians 15:55)**

YOUR THOUGHTS

SEATED LEG PRESS

READ MATTHEW 8:5-13

_M_ y husband Barry is at the gym by 6:00 a.m. every Saturday working out on the equipment. When he uses the seated leg press, his knees are bent as he readies himself to push 750 lbs.! Not bad for a 71-year-old gym rat, right? Every weekend he completes an impressive routine designed to work his muscles to exhaustion. At home he studies a color illustrated strength training book showing all the muscle groups and exercises for each of them. Every morning he hits the floor to do 100 full plank pushups. Because he is willing to study and find the time to exercise, he is physically fit for his age and maintains an ideal body weight.

As remarkable as his routine is, I am even more impressed when I see him in the morning get down on his knees next to the kitchen table, bow his head and recite The Lord's Prayer from Matthew 6:9. He mentions me, our family members, and friends with specific needs in his morning prayers. Then he gets up and reads from the Bible while he eats his cereal. Sometimes he reads me a verse that stands out to him, and we discuss it. Over time his behavior has noticeably improved with more peace and patience. His investment in prayer and Bible reading has paid off. For as long as he is living, he is learning.

Barry's trust in God's Word to produce faith in his life is exactly what Jesus commended the Roman Centurion for. The scene is documented in Matthew 8:6-10. By this time in His ministry, Jesus had a far-reaching reputation for healing the sick. People knew they could be healed if they went to Him.

When Jesus entered the city of Capernaum, the Centurion came to Jesus asking Him to heal his servant who was paralyzed. Jesus agreed and was willing to go to him. The Centurion stopped Him, though, saying he was unworthy for Jesus to visit his Gentile home. This was an incredibly humble statement for one with such high military status.

Instead, this was the officer's request: **"...just say the word, and my servant will be healed. For I, too, am a man under authority with soldiers under me. I say to this one 'Go!' and he goes, and to another 'Come!' and he comes and to my slave, 'Do this!' and he does it!'" (Matthew 8:9)**

Jesus was incredulous and commended him for his great faith. He hadn't seen such a display of belief in all Israel among the people who should have known the power of God's Word. Let me paraphrase the Centurion's confession to Jesus. "Just say the word and my servant will be healed. You don't have to be physically present with him. Your word carries all the power needed for him to be healed." He compared Jesus' words to his soldiers under him who go forth to carry out his orders. In response, Jesus commanded the servant to be healed from a distance and he was completely healed that day!

In contrast to the Centurion, the Disciples came up short in their faith. They were in a boat along with Jesus when a powerful storm suddenly arose at sea. The waves crashed against the craft, sending the Disciples to wake up Jesus who was asleep in the boat. Jesus was clearly annoyed at their panic, calling them men of little faith. He gave the command, like He had done with the Centurion, and the storm diminished. **"He replied, 'You of little faith, why are you so afraid?' then He got up and rebuked the winds and the waves, and it was completely calm. The men were amazed and asked, 'what kind of man is this? Even the winds and the waves obey Him!'" (Matthew 8:26)** Their faith was awakened as Jesus proved His authority over all nature.

Exactly what does this mean for us today? Jesus' power has never changed. He retains His authority over all nature and that authority is embodied in God's Word. Jesus does not have to be physically present to heal us and calm our storms. When we pray and read the Bible, the Holy Spirit is actively present and will implement God's power as needed.

Bible reading and prayer makes us inwardly strong and wise to deal with life's situations. Our minds are healed, corrected, and recalibrated to expect help from heaven. Living every day with that perspective, we will see God work in our natural circumstances, moving on our behalf. Like Barry's gym routine, we need to study and invest some time to see the results. Develop your own routine of Bible reading and prayer. Be consistent, holding that time as sacred. Over time, you will become stronger, have the wisdom to tackle your problems, and see answers to your prayers.

Heaven's constituents acknowledge firsthand the position of authority that Jesus holds: **"Then I heard a loud voice in Heaven say: 'Now have come the salvation and the power and the kingdom of our God, and the authority of His Christ!'"** **(Revelation 12:10)** We can join with the heavenly host to celebrate the authority of Christ by accepting Him and believing in His Word.

YOUR THOUGHTS

YOKED TOGETHER

READ MATTHEW 11:25-30

"**W**elcome to the Geauga County Fair!" This was the sign posted in front of a towering ceramic Black Angus cow wearing a red cowboy hat at the entrance of a livestock barn. The county fair was also the scene of our first date where Barry, now my husband, and I agreed to meet. The week before, he saw my profile on his feed on an "Over 50" online dating service. He liked my picture and bio and decided to message me. Employing the same dating service, I readily answered him since he seemed like a decent guy. We engaged in a lively conversation on the site and agreed to meet.

The next weekend, Labor Day, he drove an hour from a northern county in Ohio near Lake Erie and I drove an hour from a western county, converging upon a designated spot at the fair. We chatted easily as we strolled together down the fairway, past the ubiquitous fair food, settling on some beef BBQ sandwiches and fries for lunch. I enjoyed getting to know him as he generously complimented me. Most importantly during that initial rendezvous, I had to make sure that our belief in God matched. If this relationship was to lead to marriage, I could not be "unequally yoked" with someone who did not believe in Jesus. **"Do not be bound together with unbelievers; for what partnership have righteousness and lawlessness, or what fellowship has light with darkness?" (2 Corinthians 6:14)**

After lunch, we viewed the livestock, the horses, the blue-ribbon quality quilts, arts and crafts, and other agricultural wares on display. That's when we spotted the big Black Angus ceramic cow. It stood as tall as the livestock building!

We went on to watch the "Sea Lion Show." In that arena, large water tanks held two frisky sea lions that performed tricks for the crowd in exchange for raw fish from their trainer. Between the shows, we stood by the pool to have our picture taken with the sea lions as they surfaced and put their heads on our shoulders. Smile for the camera everyone!

Barry purchased a framed picture of us posing with the sea lions as a souvenir. He told me that when he saw how happy he looked in that picture, he knew I was the woman he was looking for. By the end of the day, we were talking about the possibility of marriage. The rest is wedding-bliss history!

I found out later that he was looking for a Christian woman. We both had to "yoked" to Christ before we could be equally "yoked" or joined together. Our underlying agreement to have Jesus as our life partner pre-empted choosing each other as a life partner. Here is why. People were never meant to be estranged from God, living their lives without Him. Jesus made an all-encompassing invitation to humanity to come and be "yoked" to Him. **"Come to Me, all who are weary and heavy-laden, and I will give you rest. Take my yoke upon you, and learn from Me, for I am gentle and humble in heart; and you shall find rest for your souls. For my yoke is easy and my burden is light." (Matthew 11:28-30)**

The Greek word for "yoke" is translated "to be joined to" and gives the example of the bar that connects two scales. As we join ourselves to Jesus by confession of faith in Him, He lifts the weight of our side of the scale, taking the load upon Himself. Upon that scale we find the worries and heavy-hearted cares of life are supernaturally lifted from us. We may experience hardship, but we are not overwhelmed. Barry and I have found this claim of Christ to bear out in two practical ways.

The first is the "saving rest" that God gives us. Biblical scholars agree that Jesus' appeal in Matthew was an offer to relieve people from trying to keep the Law. The futility people feel in trying to keep God's commands and failing is the very thing that points people to their need of a Savior. Instead of trying to be "good enough" to please God, people can rest in Christ's ability to satisfy God's requirement of perfection for them. Jesus was saying to people in Matthew "Come to Me and I will be your Savior." He can give us "saving rest" if we join Him by faith.

This "saving rest" was accomplished at the Cross when Jesus took the punishment for sin upon Himself. By accepting His payment for sin as our own, we are freed from the guilt of sin and death. Our confession of Christ puts us on a path towards God and away from sin. The Apostle Paul explains our "saving rest" this way: **"It was for freedom that Christ set us free; therefore, keep standing firm and do not be subject again to a yoke of slavery." (Galatians 5:1)**

Beyond that wonderful type of rest, there is also a "serving rest" that He provides. This is God's formidable power at work to serve our needs. The scripture tells us **"Cast your cares upon Him because He cares for you." (1 Peter 5:17)** Once again, Christ is pictured as the "burden bearer" who takes our worries upon Himself because He cares so deeply for our well-being.

Because He is God Almighty, Christ is willing to direct His power to serve helpless humanity. In this scripture, Christ is described as the submissive Son availing Himself to serve our needs. **"Christ Jesus, who although He existed in the form of God, did not regard equality with God as a thing to be grasped, but emptied himself, taking the form of a bondservant, and being made in the likeness of man..." (Philippians 2:5-8)**

Jesus now exerts "serving rest" to fix impossible situations that we could never solve. His power is unparalleled yet specific, perfectly measured, personal and useful. His serving power for us is the proving ground for His humility, gentleness and, most of all, His goodness.

In the Old Testament, the prophet Elisha is found by his counterpart Elijah plowing a field with twelve yoke of oxen. **"So he departed**

from there and found Elisha the son of Shaphat, while he was plowing with twelve pair of oxen before him..." (1 Kings 19:19) Elijah threw his cloak upon Elisha, calling him from his earthly plowing to be yoked with God in a supernatural miracle ministry. Twelve pairs of oxen supplied hefty muscle power to do the hard work of plowing the hard ground for planting. But now, God was calling Elisha to experience an even greater power that only God could supply, to bring healing and comfort to those experiencing hardship.

Just like that Black Angus cow that towered over the fairgoers, God's power of unmatched strength gives people "serving rest" when they rely on Him. Partnered with God, all things are possible. The sky is truly the limit. God can make things happen that people don't have the power to do. Our problems can have an unparalleled push and a supernatural shove in the right direction. We don't have to sweat it. God's "serving rest" is ours for the asking.

Barry and I believe with all our hearts that God exerted His "serving rest" on our behalf to bring two lonely "over 50" single people together in response to our cry for His help. Life is meant to be in partnership with God and with each other. We have benefited in an amazing life-changing way from being "yoked" with Jesus, and you can too!

YOUR THOUGHTS

MUDDY BOOTS

READ PSALM 69:1-3

*W*hen I bought my home, it had an inground swimming pool in the backyard. That feature was not every buyer's choice, but it certainly was mine! I love swimming and the vision of being able to jump in the water anytime during the summer months sealed the deal for me!

Once I became the homeowner, pool maintenance was rigorous. I learned how to keep the chemicals at the correct levels and keep the liner swept clean. Every year I learned a little more and the upkeep got easier. Because of my due diligence, the pool water was crystal clear and sparkling clean, transforming my backyard into a summer oasis, just like I had envisioned.

After five years of pleasurable backyard swimming, things took a "dive" downward. The Covid pandemic hit in 2020 and thousands of families installed backyard pools because they couldn't travel. Consumer demand drove the price of chemicals way up. I got married and my husband Barry, who does not like to swim, moved in with me. (Not a bad thing.) Soon, the old, weathered pool liner suffered some tearing, and its replacement cost was prohibitive. Barry and I made the tough decision to call it quits on the pool, drain the water out, remove the damaged liner, and fill up the hole with topsoil. It seemed like a gigantic undertaking, but we knew that having a lawn instead of a pool would benefit us later.

A truckload of topsoil contains seven yards of dirt, the measure used by landscape companies. We figured it would take about 12 truckloads of dirt to completely fill the pool. The first year we used three truckloads. We are now in our second year of the project. Barry has the arduous task of shoveling the dirt from our side yard into a wheelbarrow and then dumping the load into the hole in the backyard. The task of hand-shoveling all that dirt is tedious, but he is making headway.

My job is to climb into the pool wearing knee-high rubber boots and rake out the topsoil to level it. This system of shoveling and raking is working well, and we are making much progress, until we experienced heavy rain and thunderstorms for several days.

The next sunny day after the hard rain, we continued working and I got into the pool that now had a foot of water in it. I was standing on a dry pile when the dirt under me gave way and I slid into six inches of mud! It was a horrible feeling to be stuck in wet mud and sink further each time I moved. I couldn't find any solid ground to gain footing and I didn't want to step out of the boots, getting my feet and legs full of mud!

All I could do was call out to my pool partner, Barry, to ask him to give me a hand and get me out. He gladly came over and offered a strong arm to pull me and my muddy boots out of the muck. Quickly, I was freed and back on solid ground, waiting for the sun to dry up our inground marsh!

Much like I did with Barry, the Psalmist is noted for crying out to God, asking for His rescue using the same word picture as our muddy pool. **"Save me, O God, for the waters have threatened my life. I have sunk in deep mire; and there is no foothold...Deliver me from the mire; and do not let me sink..." (Psalm 69:2,14)** This person needed a life-saving measure from God to lift him out of his troubles that compared to sinking in a pit of mud.

The pervasive nature of sin within us and other people creates a complicated spiritual cesspool of problems that the Bible calls "the muck and the mire." Taken together, the combination of serious troubles, difficult emotional entanglements, offenses, lust, purposeful harm, and every other imaginable human evil comprise this murky condition that exists all around us. Jesus warned people that the potential for sinking in this awaiting cesspool resides within us.

He posed this warning when the Pharisees confronted Him, complaining that His Disciples were not following traditional, ceremonial handwashing before they ate their bread. Jesus countered their complaint by telling the religious leaders that they were transgressing God's law by not showing mercy for the sake of their own traditions. Then He publicly addressed the crowd about this confrontation, getting to the heart of the matter. **"And after He called the multitude to Him, He said to them, 'Hear and understand. Not what enters into the mouth defiles the man, but what proceeds out of the mouth, this defiles the man.'"** (Matthew 15:10-11)

His normal course of teaching was to explain to the Disciples with more clarity. **"Do you not understand that everything that goes into the mouth passes into the stomach and is eliminated. But the things that proceed out of the mouth come from the heart, and those defile the man. For out of the heart come evil thoughts, murders, adulteries, fornications, thefts, false witness, and slanders. These are the things which defile the man; but to eat with unwashed hands does not defile the man." (Matthew 15:17-20)** With this explanation, Jesus nullified the Pharisees' complaint against the Disciples omission of ceremonial handwashing and defined the underlying causes of sin.

Here is a key point from Jesus' message. We normally announce something before we do it. The thoughts of our heart float up into our mind, and the mouth speaks the words we formed in our head. Speech defiles us when we reveal the evil inclinations within our heart. For example, say someone's hate towards another person grows to the point of murder. That person will probably say, "I am going to kill that person!" If left unchecked, they will plan it out, rehearse it, and finally do it.

If they hold themselves back from the actual murder, Jesus points out that merely contemplating the act qualifies as doing it in God's sight. **"But I say to you that everyone who is angry with his brother shall be guilty before the court..." (Matthew 5:22)** People don't have to commit murder to be found guilty of murder in God's courtroom. All they need to do is say they want to do it.

The word "defile" in the Greek language means "to pollute or make something unclean." It is in the context of taking something that is holy and causing it to become profane. This can be compared to our swimming pool, holding pure, sparkling clean water and making it muddy by dumping dirt into it. Sin pollutes the innocence of our soul. It makes our soul dirty and defiled before a holy God.

One of the easiest and most common sins coming from our mouth is "murmuring," also known as grumbling or complaining. We must distinguish between occasionally voicing our dislikes from habitual, chronic railing against everything and everyone. That is the sin of murmuring that God hates and scripture addresses. **"Do all things without grumbling or disputing..." (Philippians 2:14)** The Bible says we try God's patience when we constantly voice our unequivocal unhappiness. (1 Corinthians 10: 9-10)

The Hebrew word for "grumble" means "to abide all night." In other words, we sin against God with chronic, lengthy, incessant, non-stop complaining, as if staying up all night to harp about something. When we habitually complain, we forfeit any contentment we might otherwise enjoy. We rob ourselves of peace and happiness by focusing so much on what we think is wrong instead of being grateful for what is good, beneficial, and right. Picture again my husband taking a shovel-full of dirt and dumping it into that clean pool water thousands of times. Every time we voice our complaints, we dirty our soul even more.

How do we reverse this process and dig ourselves out? We must catch ourselves by listening to the words we are saying. Do our words defile us? What is coming forth from our heart? Are we slandering people or voicing wrong actions to carry out? Process your own words in your mind, judge them according to God's Word. By God's power, stop yourself from speaking the things that defile you.

Like Barry's strong hand reaching down to pull me out of the mud, God will use His power to extricate you from habitual sin. **"I will extol Thee, O Lod, for Thou has lifted me up...Thou has kept me alive that I should not go down to the pit..." (Psalm 30:1,3)**

The Bible gives us the antidote for defilement. **"If we confess our sin, He is faithful and righteous to forgive us our sins and the cleanse us from all unrighteousness." (1 John 1:9)** As we admit our faults, our weaknesses, and our wrongdoing to God, He faithfully forgives us and, by the blood of Jesus, cleanses our soul. The defilement process is successfully reversed by our heartfelt confession and repentance. Here is a sample of the right confession from the Book of Psalms. **"Against Thee, Thee only I have I sinned, and done what is evil in They sight... Purify me with hyssop, and I shall be clean; wash me, and I shall be whiter than snow... create in me a clean heart, O God, and renew a steadfast spirit within me." (Psalm 51:4-10)**

When God cleanses our soul from the muddy mess we find ourselves in, it is permanent and life changing. We feel fresh, pure, and renewed, able to walk with clean boots going forward.

YOUR THOUGHTS

INVESTING FOR RETIREMENT

READ MATTHEW 25:31-40

_M_y husband and I believe in the value of saving for our financial security later. We are retirement age, yet we both still work. He works a full-time job and I work a part-time job along with writing and marketing my books. Fortunately, we find fulfillment in what we do for a living and the money isn't bad either. Because we plan to live well into our 90s, we have a savings goal aimed at having ample funds by then.

Planning long-term goals is an essential practice. Our youthful eyes should not be so riveted on fleeting pricey wants that we disregard the inevitable needs of our sunset years. The self-control we wield through budgeting and saving will be a blessing awaiting us someday. The plan is to be worry-free when our retirement finally comes.

Someday though, death will visit us, and we know that we will instantly be transported into God's presence. The Bible confirms, **"And inasmuch as it is appointed for men to die once and after this comes judgment."** **(Hebrews 9:27)** This implies that we will live one life and after death, face God's judgment. With such a consequential appointment looming ahead, we should apply the same principles of investing for our final retirement in heaven. Jesus gave us a snapshot of what will inevitably take place and commends us to invest ourselves in other people until that day.

Here is the unveiled description of God's final judgment of all people. **"But when the Son of Man comes in His glory, and all the angels with Him, then He will sit on His glorious throne. And all the nations will be gathered before Him... And He will separate them from one another, as the shepherd separates the sheep from the goats..."** **(Matthew 25:31-32)** In this analogy, the sheep represent righteous ones who obey God. They are regarded as righteous by their belief and faith in Jesus. They hear God's voice and follow Him. **"My sheep hear My voice, and I know them, and they follow Me..."** **(John 10:27)**

The other category of "goats" refers to the wicked. Those people are characterized as proud and stubborn in their rebellion against God. They refuse God's voice in preference to their own selfish inclinations. **"This evil people which refuse to hear my words..."** **(Jeremiah 13:10)** To stay out of this category, we need to recognize that our greatest challenge in life is having our motives right towards other people. We must rid ourselves of resenting helping others without getting anything in return. Showing mercy is non-transactional. Mercy is offered purely for the betterment of someone else who has a real need.

Let's focus on the congratulatory judgment of the "sheep." Jesus addresses those on His right. **"For I was hungry and you gave me something to eat; I was thirsty and you gave me something to drink; I was a stranger and you invited me in; naked and you clothed me; I was in prison and you came to me." (Matthew 25:35-36)** The righteous seem puzzled and ask Jesus, "When did we do all these things for You?" (Paraphrase vs 37) Their unassuming inquiry implies that they never kept track of their service on earth to receive praise or credit from others. They simply acted with mercy as situations arose.

Jesus welcomed those people into His Kingdom by virtue of His answer: **"Truly I say to you, to the extent that you did it to one of these brothers of mine, even to the least of them, you did it to Me." (vs 40)** He told them that serving others out of mercy, even for the weakest person, translates into serving God Himself. This is the meritorious lifestyle of the righteous: Serving God by serving others. How then can we invest in people for the sake of God's kingdom? Here are two types of opportunities that we will encounter. The first is short-term and momentary. The second is long-term and ongoing.

In the first instance, we may encounter unexpected requests from our own personal circle of family and friends. Someone may need a ride somewhere or help at home or with their family. You can discern if you are able to meet that need and offer them money or assistance. Other less tangible ways to invest in people are to listen to them, spend time visiting them, and letting them know that you believe in them when they face challenges. Timely encouragement can afford people the necessary push forward in their endeavors when they are too afraid to push themselves.

Group service projects such as writing letters to shut-ins and out of town college students are a wonderful way to fulfill Matthew 25: 35-36. Those handwritten notes offer solace to isolated people. Personal visits or phone calls can also brighten the lonely days of shut ins. Remember that consistent small acts of thoughtfulness add up over time.

In my book *Recipe For Sharing*, I devote a whole chapter on what I call "Hospitality To Go." This is the service of delivering meals and edible treats to homebound folks. Taking a batch of homemade soup or baked goods to someone is a wonderful way to offer condolences. It shows that you took the time to think about them.

The other avenue for investing in people is a more long-term, lifelong type of service to which God calls us. We find instructions on this in Ephesians 2:10: **"For we are His workmanship, created in Christ Jesus for good works, which God prepared beforehand, that we should walk in them."** God has preplanned a life work for each of His people. Jesus will gradually disclose this vision and give us the desire to carry it out. We need to seek Him for what He specifically has in mind.

For example, God had a plan for me to become a Christian author, although I had no formal training. As I carried out the ideas He put in my mind, I wrote and published my books. Since 1985, my writing has spanned decades and has been a life work for me. I enjoy thinking about the people who have purchased my books and hopefully received the help and answers they were seeking. Someday I will find out who they were.

Other examples of lifelong investing in people are: Christian prison ministry, full-time Christian service, affiliation and support of Christian para-church organizations, support of missionary organizations, and long-term care of others as primary caregivers for the elderly, sick or disabled. All of these and many more areas of service may be the preordained good works that God has for us.

In either category, serving others out of responsive mercy counteracts the never-ending dilemma of dire human need. Investing in others at any level avails refreshment and hope to our weary society. We can choose to live a life of giving and sharing. Although we may lose sight of what we did on behalf of someone last week or last year, those acts will be forever recorded on our ledger card when we have our appointment with Christ. Let us look forward to His words "Well done My good and faithful servant" as we invest in people now for a rich retirement someday and rest from our works.

YOUR THOUGHTS

PROM DRESSES

READ MATTHEW 9:11-17

*M*ay is the month for high school proms. I know this because I found my niche designing and sewing prom dresses, bridesmaids, and wedding gowns part-time in the 1990's. My apartment's second bedroom was set up as a sewing room filled with stacks of eveningwear fabric, patterns, and sewing supplies. Within this special occasion field, my creativity found expression and came to life. Not only did I make extra money, I also dazzled my sewing customers with the gowns they had envisioned. Oftentimes they would bring me a picture of the dress they wanted me to create for them. Many of the high school girls had very sophisticated taste for their prom dresses. I told people later that I felt like I was sewing for Cher!

One girl brought me a pattern for an off-the-shoulder gown that was knee-length in front and tapered to full-length in the back. She brought me ten yards of a rust-colored iridescent taffeta, a unique color that would stand out against all the pastel-colored dresses at the prom. The construction of the dress was unusual because the fabric had to be doubled to use as a self-lining for the see-through aspect of the short hem in front. I added an oversized bow and full-length ties to the back for extra drama. My young customer grinned happily when she came to try on the dress for the final fitting, signaling to me that I had created her dream gown!

Another girl brought me a flame-orange crepe fabric with a matching sparkly shear. She had a picture of a dress with gathered shirring up all the seams, creating tight folds across the dress. The dress had a slit up the back so she could walk, finished with a "mermaid style" gathered flounce insert using the shear fabric. We also draped the shear fabric across the neckline, the ends gathered along the short cap sleeves. The finished gown hugged her slender curves perfectly. She proudly modeled her dress for a girlfriend who came with her when she picked up the dress.

That same friend hired me to make her prom dress. This girl had gorgeous jet-black long hair and chose lipstick-red poly satin for her fabric. Again, I copied a picture of an expensive designer dress she clipped out of a glamour magazine. This gown had a small, draped cowl at the neckline in front and a more dramatic capelet that hung mid-back, gathered at the shoulder. The body of the dress had simple lines with a short, graceful train rounded in the back.

She brought her mother with her when she came to pick up the dress. Her mom started crying when she saw how beautiful her grown-up daughter looked.

The mom then turned to me and asked how much I would charge to make the exact same dress for her in royal blue? I could tell she wanted to recreate her daughter's look for herself. I looked at her and demurred because she was short and stocky with a middle-aged figure. How was I going to explain to her that the look would not be the same for her? The dress that perfectly enhanced her daughter's willowy young figure would not work as well for her. I carefully changed the subject and sent them off excited about the upcoming prom night.

Let's keep the mother/daughter scene in mind for our teaching. Referring to an old order and a new order, Jesus used the imagery of unshrunk cloth and new wine to symbolized two religious epochs now known as The Old Covenant and The New Covenant. The Law of Moses and its system of perfunctory animal sacrifice was going to be fulfilled and replaced by the sacrifice of Christ once and for all. Jesus challenged his followers to go and learn for themselves what those sacrifices represented. **"But go and learn what this means, 'I desire compassion and not sacrifice...'"** (Matthew 9:13)

He introduced John the Baptist's disciples and His own to the radically new lifestyle of following Him as their long-awaited Messiah. **"But no one puts a patch of unshrunk cloth on an old garment, for the patch pulls away from the garment, and a worse tear results." (Matthew 9:16)** Resources say that the failings of the religious system of attempting to uphold the law could not be patched and made better. Instead, it had to be replaced by a new order. The promises of the Law and the Prophets were destined to someday be fulfilled. Jesus arrived to do just that. **"Do not think that I came to abolish the Law and the Prophets; I did not come to abolish, but to fulfill."** **(Matthew 5:17)** This was like the daughter eventually growing up to outshine the mother.

Jesus goes on the combine a second analogy about new wine. **"Nor do men put new wine into old wineskins; otherwise, they wineskins burst, and the wine pours out; and the wineskins are ruined; but they put the new wine into fresh wineskins, and both are preserved."** **(Matthew 9:17)** This was like the miraculous sign at the wedding at Cana where Jesus turned water into wine and the guests exclaimed, **"Truly you have saved the best for last!"** **(John 2:1-11)** Jesus indirectly spoke of the Holy Spirit entering and infilling the human vessel. Saving the best for last, God would pour out His Spirit into human hearts, giving them the power and discernment to follow Jesus' leading throughout their daily lives. Jesus was describing a remarkable new way to live that the Old Covenant couldn't provide. The miracle at the wedding was like the daughter stepping on stage capturing everyone's attention at the prom.

The transformation we can experience by receiving the living Christ into ourselves supersedes performing rote religious activities. "Wearing" Christ like an expensive garment by acting upon the inner promptings of the Holy Spirit is how we participate in the divine nature. **"For by these He has granted to us His precious and magnificent promises; in order that by them you might become partakers of the divine nature..." (2 Peter 1:4)**

The imagery of the unshrunk cloth and the new wineskins marked the passage from the old, yet remarkable, Old Testament promises to their fulfillment in the new life in Christ. Like the splendor and excitement someone has by wearing her dream prom dress to the high school dance, we are "clothed" in the radiance of Christ and enjoy His inner presence escorting us through the dance of everyday life.

YOUR THOUGHTS

MAID OF THE MIST

READ HEBREWS 12:18-24

Witnessing the foaming panorama of Niagara Falls from the Canadian side is a scene I will never forget. The drama of all that falling water was mesmerizing. I went with a friend on a church bus trip leaving from Cleveland, Ohio years ago. Neither of us had ever been to this iconic tourist site. When the bus arrived at Falls National Park, the trip organizers gave us instructions to be back by a certain time. We all went sightseeing at our own pace. Some of the group members went to the casino to do some gambling. Others visited the park, the souvenir shops, and the food booths. My friend and I spent most of our time taking in the sights of the Falls.

We found out that Niagara Falls is the collective name for three falls— Horseshoe Falls on the Canadian side, Bridal Veil Falls in the middle, and the American Falls— the biggest waterfall in the United States. Tourist pamphlets informed us that a remarkable 600,000 gallons of water flow over the edge every second. The depth below the thunderous water is 170 feet, as deep as the gorge is high. We were fascinated by both the natural splendor and the potential for danger as we discovered more about the park's history.

Most famously were people who attempted to go over the Falls sealed inside wooden barrels. Over the years, a string of daredevils thought that they could take on the Falls and live to tell about it. The first person to survive this death-defying feat was Annie Edson Taylor in 1901. The idea of risking one's life on such a stunt is beyond me. But for some, the hypnotic power of the Falls, like a muse, beckons them to come take the ride of their life.

One of the self-guided tours we took was "Journey Behind the Falls." We rode down 150 feet in an elevator that released us to a series of well-lit tunnels. One passage led to a cave-like room behind the Falls where visitors could look out a hole in the rock to see and hear up close the rushing water crashing down. Knowing that the Niagara River flowed above us was unnerving.

After the cave tour, we went up to an observation deck where we saw people boarding the Maid of the Mist, a tourist boat that seats about 200 on an upper and lower deck. Crew members hand passengers plastic rain ponchos with hoods to wear on the voyage. We anxiously watched as the comparatively small craft inched its way out to the gorge, heading straight for the Falls. Powered by dual 350 horsepower diesel engines, the boat sailed dangerously close to the churning white water while maintaining its position against the formidable current. The passengers were duly drenched by the spray of the convulsing water.

We wondered how close the boat could go before it might be capsized by the waves. Only a seasoned boat captain would dare to take those thrill-seekers into that overpowering arena safely. Did their hearts pound as they faced the behemoth before them? Was the fear factor gleefully fun for them? Or was the close encounter with unending water too terrible to enjoy? We could only imagine their reactions as we stood observing them from afar.

We returned to the bus in time for the trip back to Cleveland, filled with an inexpressible awe from all we had seen. As we talked about our trip to folks at home, we regretted not taking the chance of boarding the Maid of the Mist ourselves.

Like those passengers on that tour boat, various people in the Bible had fantastic supernatural encounters with God and lived to tell about it. Although Jesus does not present Himself in such terrifying ways now, He is no less an unsurmountable wall of power and glory. The Book of Hebrews confirms, **"For you have not come to a mountain that may not be touched and a blazing fire, and to darkness and gloom and a whirlwind, and the blast of a trumpet and the sound of words which sound was such that those who heard begged that no further words be spoken to them. "(Hebrews 12:18-19)**

This passage refers to when Moses climbed Mt. Sinai as God's presence descended upon the mountain, appearing to set it on fire! The smoke-covered mountain shook violently as a celestial trumpet sounded. Moses traveled up the mountain to meet God at the burning bush and receive The Ten Commandments. It is recorded of Moses, **"And so terrible was the sight that Moses said, 'I am full of fear and trembling!'" (Hebrews 12:21)** This demonstration of raw supernatural power was meant to instill the fear of God in the Israelites as they lived in His presence.

Also consider the encounter that left Peter, James and John petrified as they followed Jesus up a mountain as they would often do. When they awoke from dozing off, they saw Jesus transfigured before them, becoming a glorious superhuman before their sleepy eyes. Then the long-deceased Moses and Elijah appeared and held a conversation with Jesus. **"And He was transfigured before them; and His face shone like the sun, and His garments became white as light. And behold, Moses and Elijah appeared, talking with Him." (Matthew 17:2-3)**

The three Disciples were incredulous. Only Peter dared to speak during the vision. Searching for words, he muttered something about building a tabernacle for each of the men, referring to when Moses erected a tabernacle to house the presence of God. Like the Maid of the Mist passengers tightly gripping the side railings of the boat, Peter wanted something to hold onto to secure his reeling emotions from the terror of the scene. His voice trailed off as fear overtook them and they fell on their faces before the radiance of Christ, as the voice of God the Father rang out, **"This is my beloved Son, in whom I am well-pleased; listen to Him." (Matthew 17:5)** After the vision dissipates, Jesus stood alone in his everyday clothes as before. Even so, they were forever changed after that encounter.

Years later, John is in exile on the Isle of Patmos when he is taken up into heaven by the Spirit to witness another splendid revelation of Jesus. There he sees the enthroned Christ whose appearance is dazzling. Dressed in a long white robe, His head and hair white as snow, His eyes flaming with fire. Surrounded by a glow like a furnace, His voice is the sound of many waters, perhaps like the pounding water of all of earth's waterfalls combined. John cannot bear the sight and falls down like a dead man. Jesus lifts him up saying, **"Do not be afraid; I am the First and the Last." (Revelation 1:17)** John then observes many apocalyptic visions and writes down what is yet to come.

Finally, another example of a fabulous yet frightening encounter with God is when Mary Magdalene and other women met the risen Christ after He has been crucified. **"But Mary was standing outside the tomb weeping; and so, as she wept, she stopped and looked into the tomb; and she beheld two angels in white sitting one at the head and one at the feet where the body of Jesus had been lying. And they said to her, 'Woman why are you weeping?'"** (John 20:11-23) As Mary explains her grief about not finding the body of Jesus, she turns and sees Jesus standing before her, although she does not recognize Him. He reveals Himself as He speaks her name, "Mary!" Shaken to her core, she responds "Teacher!" Jesus calms her consternation. **"Stop clinging to Me, for I have not yet ascended to the Father; but go to my brethren, and say to them, 'I ascend to My Father and your Father, and My God and your God.'"** (John 20:17) He wanted her to know that the power she was witnessing had been wielded on her behalf and she need not be afraid of Him.

From these amazing scenes that reveal the daunting power of God, we can breathe a sigh of relief. Even with frightful manifestations of Jesus, we should not run from Him. Like the Maid of the Mist bravely making its way out to the Falls, we need to move towards God, not away from Him. We can experience His measured power as He helps us, hear His quiet voice as He guides us and know His touch when He lifts us up.

Although we need not be afraid of God, we should remember these examples and have a healthy awe and respect for the enthroned Christ. **"Therefore, since we receive a kingdom which cannot be shaken, let us show gratitude by which we may offer to God an acceptable service with reverence and awe." (Hebrews 12:28)** Keeping these glorious excerpts from the Bible in mind, we can come boldly before the throne of God. Christ has reconciled us with God the Father so that we can claim "My Father, My God" with certainty instead of fear.

YOUR THOUGHTS

PAY PHONES

READ LUKE 11:1-4

C oin-operated pay phones, like pre-historic dinosaurs, maintain a lingering presence in quaint towns such as Chillicothe, Ohio where this picture was taken. Before mobile cell phones became prevalent, pay phones were available for public use at busy intersections, gas stations, and inside buildings. They afforded people valuable communication services outside the home. If someone ran out of gas or had to make an urgent call, they could easily find a pay phone to call for help.

Dating back to the early 1900s, over 80,000 pay phones dotted the United States by 1902. By 1960, the Bell System installed its millionth telephone booth for consumer use. The cost to make a phone call in 1950 was a nickel, a dime by 1980 and after that, the cost increased to a quarter. Originally the calls were put through by myriads of switchboard operators until those folks were replaced by the system of direct dial. By now, most major phone carriers have abandoned the pay phone business, although some may still exist.

The pay phone is the image used here as a symbol of the ancient practice of prayer, although prayer will never become obsolete. Throughout the centuries, prayer has been the direct "dial up" to immediately put us in touch with heaven. With prayer, we have life-saving access to God's help 24/7. **"He who keeps you will not slumber or sleep." (Psalm 121:3)** People call upon God because they believe that He hears, and He will answer them. In their distress, they can ask for God's help and be assured that He will make a way for them.

The Bible mentions many nuances of prayer. I will share three aspects that are invariably helpful. They are 1) prayer as a means of learning dependence upon God 2) prayer as a means of personal growth 3) prayer as a source of community service and healing.

The basics of prayer are taught in Luke 11:1 where we find the Disciples observing Jesus as He prays. After He finished, they approached Him and said, **"Lord, teach us to pray just as John taught his disciples." (Luke 11:1)** Jesus gave a template for prayer in Luke 11:2-4 that we can personalize and expand upon. This passage is commonly known as "The Lord's Prayer" or "The Our Father Prayer." Briefly, these words acknowledge the Father's holiness and our request for the purity of His will. It shows us to ask for daily sustenance, forgiveness of sin, help with the forgiveness of others, and a plea to keep us off the path of evil. People looking to increase their discipline in prayer should pray "The Lord's Prayer" often because it covers our primary needs.

No one should be at a loss for words or embarrassed about not knowing how to pray. Prayer is a practice that we can learn. In addition to this prayer model, we will find our own words to say to God, and those words will be well-received. We can easily talk to God even silently in our hearts.

The goal of prayer is to transfer dependency off ourselves and onto God. That may take some time because we naturally want to stay in control of our earthly affairs. When we condition ourselves to pray about mostly everything, the result is transformative. **"Be anxious for nothing, but in everything by prayer and supplication with thanksgiving, let your requests be made known to God." (Philippians 4:6)** Jesus assured us that God will give us His best when He answers our prayers. **"If you, then, being evil, know how to give good gifts to your children, how much more shall your father who is in Heaven give what is good to those who ask Him?" (Matthew 7:11)** Believing this is true, we should wean ourselves off the fear of letting go and allow God to furnish our needs perfectly.

As we continually practice prayer, we avail ourselves to the second aspect, which is personal growth. Staying in contact with God familiarizes us with the sense of His presence. Knowing we have an audience with Him, we can speak to Him about deeply personal concerns. We will receive answers as He speaks to our mind and through the words of scripture.

We will make wiser decisions in life when we gain heavenly perspectives through divine guidance. Rising higher from our self-centered point of view transforms us into thoughtful, congenial adults. We shed immature personality traits as God shows us the full scope of life and what is worth living for. As selfishness loosens its enticing grip on our soul, we start to truly care about other people and take up their concerns through prayer. **"Therefore, confess your sins to one another, and pray for one another, so that you may be healed."** (James 5:16) Physical and emotional healing comes from opening ourselves up to God and to others. Honesty and transparency free our minds and hearts from self-centered postures.

One critical attribute of personal growth is replacing retaliation against others with prayer for them. Convincing ourselves to forgive those who have harmed us and pivoting to pray for them is a huge step in character growth. **"See to it that no one repays another with evil for evil, but always seek after that which is good for one another and for all men. Rejoice always, pray without ceasing; in everything give thanks; for this is God's will for you in Christ Jesus."** (1 Thessalonians 5:15-18) There are several directives in this passage that are bundled together with prayer as the facilitator of them all.

Jesus took the lead on this higher road by negating the retribution prayers of the Old Testament. Rather than asking God to punish or even kill our enemies, Jesus commanded us to love and pray for our enemies, that they would taste God's grace and turn from evil. **"You have heard that it was said, 'You shall love your neighbor and hate your enemy. But I say to you, love your enemies, and** pray for those who persecute you.'" (Matthew 5:43-44) This may seem like a stretch for most of us, but the power of prayer enables us to do things that we cannot ordinarily do.

Fortunately, the safeguard of any misguided prayers is under the auspicious control of God Himself. The Book of Revelation pictures the actual place where our prayers ascend. **"And another angel came and stood at the altar, holding a golden censor; and much incense was given to him, that he might add it to the prayers of all the saints upon the golden altar which was before the throne. And the smoke of the incense, with the prayers of all the saints, went up before God out of the angel's hand."** (Revelation 8:3-4)

To put this in context, Moses built the earthly replica of the altar before God's throne at the time of the tabernacle in the desert. God told him to build everything exactly as He showed him to make a place on earth as it was in heaven. That was the place God could indwell. The priests who ministered before the Lord mixed sweet incense and then placed it in firepans on the golden altar. There it was burned up by hot coals. This was the Old Testament picture of prayer. **"And he shall take a firepan full of coals of fire from the altar before the Lord and two handfuls of finely ground sweet incense and bring it inside the veil."** (Leviticus 16:12) Resources say that the fiery coals in heaven purify our prayers by burning off wrong motives and our attempts to use prayer for vindictive purposes.

The collective prayers of mankind burning day and night before God are contained in a type of "cauldron of good" that God uses to send protection and healing to earth. This is not a mystical concept because the historical tabernacle of Moses matched the golden altar that John saw in his vision of God's throne. By God's will, people around the world receive answers to prayer, healing, and miracles due to the incense of believers' prayers.

This leads us to the third aspect of prayer that casts a vision for us to engage in community service through collective prayer. This type of prayer is called "intercession." God holds us responsible for crying out to Him asking for national healing. **"And He said to them, 'Is it not written, 'My house shall be called a House of Prayer for all the nations?'" (Mark 11:17)**

Thus far, we have covered how we call out to God in prayer. Like our pay phone example, sometimes we are on the receiving end as God calls on us to pray. When this happens, we will experience an urge to pray within us at a specific moment in time. We will have a sense that we need to pray.

I will finish with a dramatic example of intercession that happened to me. Deep in the middle of the night on April 15, 2013, I woke to God's voice urgently saying, "Pray!" I obeyed and used my prayer language to go into intercession as described in scripture. **"...for we do not know how to pray as we should, but the Spirit Himself intercedes for us with groanings too deep for words..." (Romans 8:26)** I could feel the Holy Spirit's power coursing through me. I was probably in prayer for about five hours until the feeling subsided. I got up from bed at my normal 7:00 a.m. time to go to work even though I was exhausted. After work, I ate dinner and changed into my gym clothes to go workout at the gym. While I was walking on the treadmill, I watched the evening news on the television screens mounted on the gym wall. Although I could not hear the sound, I saw scenes of a bombing shown repeatedly. I thought to myself, *"Are these scenes of a war zone somewhere?"*

Finally, the news printed on the screen revealed that two homemade bombs had gone off near the finish line at the 2013 Boston Marathon. Instantly I knew this was the event I was praying about throughout the night. Two terrorist brothers planted homemade pressure-cooker bombs filled with shrapnel with timing devices near the finish line. They left them in knapsacks and casually walked away, as street cameras recorded their moves.

At approximately 2:50 p.m., runners were crossing the finish line as the thunderous sound of an explosion shook the area. Minutes later the second bomb went off. People who were not hit by the flying shrapnel scrambled from the scene. Victims of the bombs lay in the street until good Samaritans and EMT's could reach them to apply tourniquets to stop the bleeding.

Miraculously, only three people were killed from the blasts even though 266 were injured. Some lost limbs, some lost eyesight and others almost bled to death. Even so, one reporter noted, "There should have been more deaths outside the forum, but much of the blast (of the second bomb) had been contained and halted by a large postal box that was bolted into the ground."[4] As families were reunited with loved ones who had not been hurt, "Oh Thank God! Thank God!" was a common refrain as families found their runners. [5] It was a miracle that more people were not killed.

---

4. *Boston Strong*, P. 73
5. Ibid, P. 106

I went home shaken after finding out what had happened in Boston that day. Somehow God had called me up to intercede for that forthcoming disaster. There have been other occasions when God has called me in the middle of the night to pray. The outcome of those situations has not been disclosed to me. As a result, I take God's calling of intercession very seriously. I know that He watches the earth, looking for places to intervene and I want to participate in that beautiful, sweet incense of prayer for the healing of the nations.

This is one of my favorite verses in the Bible letting us know that, because of prayer, God is actively at work in people's lives to bring answers to prayer. **"And it shall come to pass that before they call, I will answer; and while they are still speaking, I will hear."** **(Isaiah 65:24)** That is the result of prayer—that we can know God is working things out for the good of those who seek Him. Prayer is powerful because God Himself is powerful. We can see direct results of our persistent prayers and realize that in all circumstances, God knows, and He cares.

YOUR THOUGHTS

FRESH TROUT

READ JOHN 21:1-14

*F*resh trout, sauteed in garlic butter with a side hash browns. That was my selection from the breakfast menu when I visited Colorado with a ministry group years ago. I was struck by how different the landscape was there compared to my home state of Ohio. From the city of Colorado Springs, there were snow-capped mountains permanently occupying the horizon from every vantage point. That terrain produces mountain streams, rivers, and lakes known for some of the best trout fishing in the country.

According to the state website, there are 9,000 miles of fishable areas statewide. Over 320 are "Gold Medal" waters, a unique award designating highly abundant fishing spots that can produce 60 lbs. of trout per acre. It is almost impossible to NOT catch a trout when fishing in those waters!

The restaurant server brought our meals, and I was delighted with the flaky, white meat and sweet, delicate taste of my trout breakfast. I thought to myself, *"Why not try something native to the area?"* That was my way of taking a personal memory home with me to Ohio.

So memorable, in fact, that I recalled that experience years later when I hosted a couple one summer for Sunday brunch. The husband was an avid hunter, handily downing a deer most hunting seasons and freezing the meat for meals. What could I serve this couple who had an affinity for game? Fresh trout, of course! I planned for an outdoors theme and purchased the fish from the grocery store.

The couple arrived for brunch, and I led them to my back deck to sit outdoors. Planter boxes and flowerpots surrounded us on three sides, all filled with colorful blooms. A multi-color patio umbrella was secured in the middle of the glass table, shading us from the morning sun. I served them a fruit plate with yogurt and some cheese and crackers along with hot coffee. Then I ducked inside to pan fry the fish and the hash browns. I had since learned to cut the fish head off before frying. The fish was already gutted and scaled. I simply fried both sides in butter until the fish turned white throughout. I melted some extra butter with fresh garlic and parsley. When the fish was done, I removed it from the pan and used a sharp knife to lift the backbone along with the skeleton out in one piece. I poured on the melted garlic butter and served each dish with hash browns, just like my breakfast in Colorado!

My friends were genuinely endeared that I carried out the game theme just for them. The menu reminded them of many hunting and fishing stories that I found fascinating. My hope in planning this hospitality event was to humbly serve my guests in a way that was personal for them.

Personally serving His beloved friends was Jesus' motive when He remarkably appeared to the Disciples after His resurrection and prepared for them a fresh-catch breakfast. The Bible recounts that Jesus chose to manifest Himself to them before He ascended to heaven. The day before, Simon-Peter told the group, "I'm going fishing." They all decided to go with him. They fished all night and caught nothing. At daybreak, they looked back to the shore and saw a man waving to them but did not recognize Him. Jesus called out to them, "Did you catch anything?" They answered, "No, nothing." Jesus told them to cast their net on the opposite side of the boat and they obliged. Immediately, they caught a great number of fish, as if Jesus transformed the lake into "Gold Medal" waters just for them! They caught so many fish that they couldn't haul them all in at one time.

John, the beloved disciple looked at all the fish and then looked at the man grinning on shore. "It is the Lord!" he said to Peter. Their hearts raced as they recognized the risen Christ, standing on the shore with His arms out to them.

Unfazed by the miracle, Jesus said to them, **"Bring some of the fish which you have now caught." (John 21:10)** Jesus had a fire going for cooking along with some bread. He prepared breakfast for them and invited them to eat. **"Come and have breakfast." (vs 12)** One by one, the incredulous Disciples gathered around the risen Christ as He casually served them their food. They relished the fresh catch and being reunited with Jesus, for which there were no words.

Jesus had appeared to the Disciples one other time in a more unearthly way. They were gathered in a locked room when Jesus suddenly appeared and stood among them. He spoke to allay their fright. **"Jesus came and stood in their midst, and said to them, 'Peace be with you.'" (John 20:19)** Love and relationship preempted their understandable fear.

In the same way, we are enrapt by His presence in our lives. The risen Christ works on our behalf to bring us His abundant life. His resurrection power lifts our daily mundane routine from dull to dazzling; from "ho-him" to humbling. He continues to serve us with personal experiences that speak to us and build our belief in Him.

That huge catch of fish that Jesus miraculously produced spoke intensely to those fishermen who had worked all night and caught nothing. Like the Disciples, we don't have a mystical, magical Christ floating around unconnected to our world and unfamiliar with our concerns. Indeed, we have a personal, loving Christ who is well acquainted with our weaknesses, fears, and basic needs. He reveals His love in practical, useful ways, making our lives better, enriching us, and providing for us.

Jesus told us the terms of this consequential relationship with Him. **"Whoever has My commands and obeys them, he is the one who loves me. He who loves me will be loved by my Father, and I too will love him and show myself to him." (John 14:21)** Like the fishermen who obeyed the command of Jesus to lower their net on the other side, we need to open ourselves to the directives of Christ and not rely on our own reasoning to figure things out. We need to convince ourselves that the risen Christ knows better than us.

As a result, when some unexpected gift comes your way, give God credit for what He does for you. Don't take good fortune for granted. Say to yourself, "*It is the Lord!*" Certainly, be amazed at His timely touch. But more importantly, be humble and grateful that He chooses to manifest Himself to each of us in a personal way.

YOUR THOUGHTS

HIKING IN HINCKLEY

READ JOHN 8:31-36

*H*inkley, Ohio is a small township located about 25 miles south of Cleveland. At a glance, it is home to cabin-like residences tucked away within a densely wooded landscape. The Cleveland MetroParks has aptly extended its parks system to include Hinckley Reservation. This 2,800-acre tract is laced with 26 miles of hiking trails and six miles of horse-riding trails. The public park offers swimming and canoeing in the pristine waters of Hinckley Reservoir Lake. Adjacent to the reservoir is Whipp's Ledges, where adventurous visitors can climb well-marked rocky paths that ascend 350 feet above the lake. Wherever they go, outdoor types can find plenty of room to run and play among the numerous picnic groves, ball fields and open grassy meadows.

Another draw for Hinkley Reservation is a spot called "Buzzard Roost." This corner of the park is locally celebrated for buzzards that come here to roost and mate every spring. Nature lovers gather at this site to view the buzzards flying in to complete their annual northern migration. The buzzards are turkey vultures which, unlike other birds of their species, don't kill their prey. Instead, they consume the existing dead animals they find.

The migration pattern of these birds was first discovered in 1957 by a local news reporter. He tracked the arrival of the birds for 30 years and found them true to their Hinckley destination every March 15th. After this remarkable finding was reported, the Chamber of Commerce marketed the sightings as its claim to fame. Hinkley is now undoubtedly known throughout northern Ohio as "the home of the buzzards."

Aware of these amenities, I planned a day for my husband and me to hike the trails of Hinkley one Saturday in July. Driving south, we found the park entrance near the reservoir. We parked near the boathouse where the canoe rental was. Across from the boat dock we saw a map posting all the hiking trails including Whipp's Ledges. We decided to go on a five-mile hike encircling the lake and easily found the path markings to follow.

The sights and sounds of Hinckley did not disappoint. We gazed across the lake, shimmering in the sunlight, and saw paddleboats, canoes and kayaks lazily making their voyages. At the tip of the lake, we enjoyed the seclusion of the marshes and emerged into a canopy of long-established woods. Ending our five miles, we crossed at the causeway where the reservoir gently spills over into a retaining pond. There, children splash in the cool, shallow water, catch minnows, and play with buckets of sand.

As we walked the remainder of the trail, I looked down and saw a small, brown snake writhing on the path near my foot. Instinctively, I let out a gut-level scream.

"What's wrong?" Barry said, coming to my rescue.

"There's a snake on the trail!" I squealed. He was worried because I had let out a scream like I had been attacked by an anaconda!

"It's just a small woods snake. It won't hurt you," he said calmly.

That was true, but I was immersed in fear at that moment. I dutifully warned other hikers who we met going the other direction to be careful of the snake on the path! I finally settled down, realizing that my fear was unfounded, looming larger than the threat the snake actually posed.

Admittedly, the small snake was not an anaconda. Unlike buzzards, anacondas aren't indigenous to Ohio. They make their home in the swamps of South America, not on the hiking trails of Hinkley. Unlike some species of snakes, anacondas don't bite and inject poisonous venom into their prey. Instead, they wrap their, possibly 17 feet, 200 lb., bodies around their victim and strangle it to death. I reacted like I encountered an anaconda instead of a small, harmless woods snake, like Barry said.

We finished our hike and arrived at our car with no further incidents. Regardless of the critters we discovered in nature, we were delighted by the idyllic scenes of Hinckley.

Let's use the image of that carefree stroll in the woods to understand the figurative language that Jesus used to convince His followers to trust in Him and be free from fear. He began by promising freedom to His Disciples. **"If you abide in my word, then you are truly disciples of mine; and you shall know the truth, and the truth shall make you free." (John 8:31)** This statement begs the question; Free from what? We can be free from the basis of all fear, which is the fear of death. The Word of God explains how to have that freedom. By believing in Christ's death on the Cross that conquered sin and death on our behalf, we can look to Jesus for the payment for our sin. Accepting His sacrifice releases us from guilt, punishment, and the fear of eternal death. Christ's resurrection proves that death no longer has a hold on us. Although we die, we live again in Christ.

Jesus concluded, **"If therefore, the Son shall make you free, you shall be free indeed." (John 8:36)** Because of Jesus, we are set free from slavery to sin and no longer must obey it. Instead, we follow the commands of Jesus and choose the path, like the well-marked trails of Hinkley. We walk away from sin and walk unhindered towards God.

The fear of death is the basis for all other fears we may have, real or imagined. If that basic fear is conquered by the assurance of life in Christ, then every other fear is a lesser fear and potentially vanquished. Again, let's picture the anaconda. It is a huge snake, in a class all its own. This represents the grip that the fear of death has on the human psyche. There is nothing that constricts our thinking and movement like deep-seated fear. It stops us in our tracks, immobilizing us from the most mundane activities. When fear visits, panic makes us gasp for breath like we are being suffocated.

Belief in Jesus breaks the bondage to fear. The invasive voice that says, "What if the worst happens to you?" no longer haunts your mind. It trails off as a faint, inaudible whisper while the assurance of God's love takes control. Then we can rationally distinguish between what is life-threatening and what is not. The dark clouds of doom and gloom give way to a life of hope-filled possibilities.

Jesus continued His case against fear by referring to Himself as "The Gate." **"Jesus therefore said to them again, 'Truly, truly I say to you, I am the gate for the sheep... I am the gate; if anyone enters through Me, he shall be saved, and shall go in and out and find pasture.'" (John 10:7-9)** His figurative language is a word picture describing well-protected sheep, coming and going as they please, finding safe pasture to roam and graze. This is like the liberty we experienced on our hike in Hinkley. We were out in the open air with no cares, no threats, and free to be ourselves! That is God's goal for us— to experience His unequivocal love, safety, and care. To love us is to take good care of us, and He does that perfectly!

The psalmist celebrates the absence of fear that comes from trusting in God. **"The Lord is the defense of my life; whom shall I dread?" (Psalm 27:1)** The Apostle Paul restates the freedom from fear that he found in Christ. **"For I am convinced that neither death, nor life, nor angels, nor principalities, nor things present, nor things to come, nor powers, nor heights, nor depth, nor any other created thing shall be able to separate us from the love of God which is in Christ Jesus our Lord." (Romans 8:38-39)** Nothing and no one can make us afraid because God's love overpowers it all. We are not constricted nor constrained. Our hearts are free, and we can walk fearlessly. **"For God has not given us a spirit of fear, but of power and love, and discipline."** **(2 Timothy 1:7)** God will empower us to push through debilitating fears, seeing them as small wood snakes instead of giant anacondas. He wants us to step out onto the trails He marks out for us and follow them to the destination He has envisioned. This is how we live in Christ: in freedom, unafraid, and on a sure path. We will surely marvel at what He shows us along the way.

YOUR THOUGHTS

GATORS ON THE GOLF COURSE

READ MATTHEW 13:24-30

*I*n 1995, my mom and I drove from Cleveland, Ohio to Ft. Myers, Florida to visit a retired couple who were our next-door neighbors when I was growing up. They moved from Ohio to build a new home in Ft. Myers within a golf course community where the homes encircled the course. When we arrived, they gave us a tour and showed us the dents in the siding from misguided golf balls hitting the house.

We visited during the Thanksgiving holiday, and I had the blissful pleasure of swimming in one of the community pools on Thanksgiving morning, something unheard of in Ohio. Later in the day, our friends treated us to a full-course turkey dinner served at the country club restaurant.

For four days we made trips to the white beaches of Ft. Myers beach to swim in the Gulf of Mexico. One day my mom and I drove across the causeway to Sanibel Island where we poked around in trendy shops and found a place to have lunch. We discovered that water, sand, and sun were the signature elements of Florida.

Unfortunately, those same elements are the favorite habitat for alligators. Our neighbors warned us not to sightsee near the canals or golf course ponds where alligators could be living. In Florida, nuisance alligators over four feet long sometimes sun themselves on canal banks or stroll on the greens of golf courses. Golf courses are hot spots for gators due to the well-maintained ponds that are often stocked with fish. Florida has the second largest population of alligators in any U.S. state. Except in the salty ocean, these reptiles can be found living in Florida anywhere there is a large body of water.

For some interesting golf trivia, in 2017 a golfer prodded a slumbering gator off the fairway and into the water during the opening of the Arnold Palmer Invitational in Orlando, Florida. The internet is full of stories about gators wandering around on golf courses and swimming in residential swimming pools!

In general, alligators are opportunistic predators that eat whatever is the easiest prey. Sometimes they float on the surface of the water, perfectly still and appearing like a floating log. Any unsuspecting bird, turtle, frog, or small animal may hop onto the "log" and wind up caught in the alligator's quick jaws. To a large gator, any animal coming to drink from the water bank could be fair game. Once an alligator catches its prey, the biting force of its jaws crushes the animal. The bite force of a 12-foot, 450 lb. alligator has been measured to be 2,200 lbs., making the reptile a formidable enemy.

People are not an alligator's natural prey. However, golfers, hikers and unwary tourists in Florida need to have a healthy caution for any gator that appears in their path.

Now that we have been forewarned of the possible perils of golfing in Florida, let's use this image from the wild to talk about a life-saving instinct called "discernment." The word "discern" is derived from the Latin words *dis* which means "apart" and *cernere* which means "to separate." It means to clearly recognize or differentiate. Discernment does not involve the physical separation of two tangible objects, but rather the mental ability to distinguish between two entities or concepts even though they may be combined as one. Our minds can sort out the components that make up the whole of something. Discernment is also the identification of the true nature of something that may be hidden from full view.

For the Christian, this includes the spiritual ability to have God's perspective, insight, and divine wisdom that supersedes our own natural senses. It is a type of "seeing" that the Holy Spirit provides. Many times, discernment comes to us not with words, but as a "gut" instinct telling us something isn't right. We experience an inner alarm going off, warning us of danger or deception.

In our daily living we apply discernment to relationships with people who do not have the right motives towards us. They may appear to be friendly or helpful, like the alligator posing as a floating log in the water. When the time is ripe, we find out that they are only trying to take advantage of us through some devious means, scam or reuse. These human "alligators" could be both friends or strangers depending on who we let into our inner circle.

People can break trust with others due to their self-serving motives. To our face, they are a friend, but behind our back, they are an enemy i.e. "frienemy." Their proximity positions them to do us harm. People can express their ill-will through gossip, backbiting, and false reports about us. Like the unsuspecting bird, turtle, or frog, we may get caught in the jaws of such a person and feel the crushing weight of their words against us.

In Matthew 13:24-30 Jesus introduces discernment to His followers by telling the parable of the wheat and tares. He warns of the evil motives of people by describing the world as a wheat field. In the parable, a man sowed a field with kernels of wheat, fully expecting a good harvest for his efforts. While the man was asleep, an enemy purposefully sowed seeds that would grow tares or weeds. The plants grew and the man realized that his wheat field was ruined by weeds, to his disappointment. Bewildered, he asks if he should pull out the weeds growing amid the wheat?

Jesus finished the story by saying, **"No, lest while you are gathering up the tares, you may root up the wheat with them. Allow both to grow together until the harvest." (Matthew 13; 24-30)** At harvest time, the weeds would be bundled together and thrown into the fire. Then the wheat would be harvested and taken into the barns.

The field of wheat represents our world full of people. Everyone has an opportunity to be responsible, productive citizens, yielding their respective contributions to society. That is the wheat, and the harvest is a well-lived life. Unfortunately, the devil comes to people and entices their minds with lies, get-rich schemes and self-serving motives that can accost others. These people are the "tares" whose deceptive, predatory actions are counterproductive, if not illegal. They cause trouble for other people who are innocently trying to make a way in life.

We cannot see into other people's hearts and know what their endgame is. We must rely upon God to see people's motives towards us and warn us if anyone is trying to deceive us. God will expose the "alligators" roaming around looking for whomever they may devour.

God does not want people to be ignorant, naïve, or unequipped to live in a fallen world under the influence of the devil. We must trust God to give us discernment as we interact with people. **"My prayer is not that you take them out of the world, but that you protect them from the evil one." (John 17:15)**

Although widespread malice exists, it is not good for us to adopt a suspicious, cynical outlook, thinking that everyone is out to get us. Sprinkled along our path we will also find good, genuine people who are kind-hearted and willing to help. We must be able to discern both. Good-hearted people are a pleasure to get to know.

Most importantly, we need to know our own hearts and examine our own motives towards others. **"Behold, I send you out as sheep in the midst of wolves; therefore, be shrewd as serpents, and innocent as doves." (Matthew 10:16)** We need to stop ourselves from getting into the "weeds" of gossip and drama. Make sure you do not put on a façade to look good to others while letting your motives go unchecked. Be genuine and honest in your relationships, taking strides towards self-improvement.

Finally, when we are actively doing God's will and accomplishing the work He has for us, that work will occupy us. We won't have time to become distracted and "major in the minors." We will disregard petty scheming and choose to live higher by staying out of the "weeds" that we discern.

YOUR THOUGHTS

THE DOOR KNOCKER

READ 1 CORINTHIANS 16:5-10

Whrning repairs to my home, I had a new front door installed. I also removed the broken doorbell and replaced it with a door knocker instead. The nickel-plated door knocker I purchased had a flat plate on it that was well-suited for engraving. I took it to a gift shop at the mall and had the words "Thy Will Be Done" engraved onto the plate. My repairman mounted the door knocker onto the door, thereby distinguishing my home as one dedicated to the will of God.

When Barry and I were married, he moved into my home with me. We agreed to live in devotion to God's will, just like our door knocker claimed. Settling into our routine now, I sometimes catch him off-guard with my impulsive decisions.

A woman at our church approached me to ask if Barry and I would like to join the Chimes Choir for an upcoming Easter season service. Without hesitating I said, "Yes!" though I was fully aware that Barry and I are not musical people. We can barely carry a tune, we don't play instruments, and we can't read music. That is why he was surprised when I told him about our performing in the choir.

"Why are you volunteering us?" he asked after our names were added to the list. "We don't know how to do that!"

"I know," I said. "But it will be fun to join, and we will learn something new!"

We dutifully showed up at the first rehearsal and the music leader assigned us our hand chimes. I had two chimes to play, with notes in most of the song. Barry had one lower range note to play a couple times at the end. As members took their places, we both stood next to someone who could read music and help us if we got lost during the song. We took the sheet music home to practice counting notes while tapping on the kitchen table. "One, two, three, four. One... Two..."

After plenty of rehearsals, the Chimes Choir was ready to play their song. Easter Sunday morning we performed the hymn *Jesus Christ Has Risen Today* before the congregation. Barry and I could be seen nodding our heads up and down, keeping time and counting notes to ourselves. "One, two, three, four. One...Two..." We successfully rang our chimes at the right time, holding the last vibrating note for a big finish at the end! We were met with applause! The special music featuring chimes added a unique element to the worship service that everyone enjoyed.

Afterwards during coffee hour, the music director showed me a video of a community performance of Handel's *Messiah* in which she participated. She played an instrument in the orchestra. Every year, worshipers from around the city meet at a large church on Cleveland's West Side to sing Handel's *Messiah*. She said it took about two hours to perform the whole piece. I watched the short recording of local talent singing their respective parts from sheet music that was provided. No rehearsals for this one— people just showed up and sang!

"We are going to do that next year!" I said emphatically.

Barry heard me and rolled his eyes. "I can't wait," he said.

Was that sarcasm? I'm not sure. It doesn't really matter because I made up my mind to do it!

His question to me later was, why do I volunteer for events that we have no training in?

I do it because of the message on our door knocker, "Thy Will Be Done." Let's take a closer look at the scripture verse from which this phrase was extracted. **"Thy Kingdom come; thy will be done on earth as it is in heaven." (Matthew 6:10)** This says that it is God's will to make earth as heavenly as possible. If we believe that, then we need to be available to bring heaven in by doing the Father's will.

The Bible says that Jesus stands at the door of our heart and knocks. **"Behold, I stand at the door and knock; if anyone hears my voice and opens the door, I will come into Him and dine with**

him and he with Me." (Revelation 3:20) Before He said this, He encouraged people to **"be zealous" (vs 19)** or enthusiastic about God approaching them. To "dine" with Him means to share a meal together eating food.

During His ministry, Jesus said, **"My food is to do the will of Him who sent Me, and to accomplish His work." (John 4: 34)** When Jesus approaches us with a "knock" on our heart, it is an invitation to join Him in accomplishing God's will on earth. He will show us some act of service that glorifies God, making Him known to other people. This could be a variety of activities and opens us up to doing things we have never done before. When we "dine" with Jesus, we must rely on God to provide the talent and the power to meet His challenge. These tasks may be a stretch for us. Regardless, be zealous and accept His challenge eagerly. He will provide the way and means to do it. If we give God our availability, then He will give us His ability.

This is the vibrancy of the Christian life. We never become stagnant in our daily routines. Instead, we learn new skills and perform tasks we never thought of doing, just like Barry and I did in the Chimes Choir. Like our front door knocker, when we stay open to Jesus "knocking" on our heart, God can open new doors for far-reaching service. The Apostle Paul told the church at Corinth, **"for a wide door for effective service has opened to me." (1 Corinthians 16: 9)** God will open doors of opportunity for us when we keep the door of our heart open to Him.

Let me finish with the example of Handel's *Messiah*. In London England, 1741, Charles Jennens handed composer George Frederic Handel a *libretto* of words intended for an Easter service the following year. The words penned by the literary scholar were carefully selected Old and New Testament scriptures documenting prophecies about the Messiah, Jesus' birth, death on the cross and the resurrection. He hoped that Handel's genius and skill would produce a composition that would exceed all his other works. This was the "knock" on Handel's heart.

Handel took the challenge and, in an astounding interlude, composed *Messiah* in just three to four weeks. Many believed it was divinely inspired because Jesus was "dining" with him in a supernatural visitation. It is told that Handel never left the house during those weeks and a friend who visited discovered him sobbing with intense emotion, seemingly overwhelmed by the presence of God. After he wrote the *Hallelujah Chorus*, Handel was quoted as saying, "I did think I did saw all Heaven before me, and the Great God Himself."

For Jennens and Handel, *Messiah* became an evangelistic tool to share the Gospel with the masses. The finished work made its debut in Dublin, Ireland, a prosperous European city at the time. *Messiah's* success in Dublin was quickly repeated back in London. Eventually the piece became a Christmas favorite. By the nineteenth century, performances of *Messiah* became an even stronger Christmas tradition in the United States than in England.

Performances in Handel's day were often benefit concerts to help release people from debtors' prison or feed orphans. One scholar wrote, "*Messiah* has fed the hungry, clothed the naked and fostered the orphan more than any single musical production in this or any other country." However, George Frederic Handel did not want any of the credit.

Why would he not take credit for his renowned composition? Because he knew it was not him, but God who gave him all the skill and inspiration to write that heavenly music. **"On earth as it is in heaven."** Handel was given a wide door by God for effective service that goes on to this day. Barry and I are going celebrate that wide door by singing along next year!

"I stand at the door and knock." Jesus wants to do the Father's will on the earth— to make earth as heavenly as possible. He continues to knock on hearts to do that. Will you listen to His voice and open the door to a greater work that you normally can't do? Why not *you*? Why not *now*?

YOUR THOUGHTS

THE BILTMORE

READ REVELATION 22:10-24

*T*he year 1892 was the height of the Guilded Age in American history, an era marked by unprecedented wealth belonging to a forward-looking group of entrepreneurs. At least 100 millionaires acquired fortunes exceeding $10 million dollars, an unheard-of sum of money at that time. It was estimated that nine percent of American families controlled 71 percent of the nation's wealth. [6]

One of the most colorful and well-known families of this upper class was the Vanderbilt family. Patriarch Cornelius Vanderbilt, also known as The Commodore, began his career in the shipping industry

---

6. *Fortune's Children*, P. 264

carrying passengers on a ferryboat from the New York harbor. Later in life, he expanded his enterprise to railroads. After a lifetime of ambitious business dealings, he amassed a personal fortune of $105 million. At age 83, he was richer by far than anyone in the United States. [7] The Commodore died in 1877, leaving his vast wealth to two sons, eight daughters, 16 grandsons, and 17 granddaughters. [8]

In the winter of 1888, the 26-year-old grandson, George Vanderbilt, traveled with his mother to the Great Smoky Mountains of North Carolina for relief from the harsh cold of New York City. George was inspired by the majesty of the area and envisioned building a retreat home near the mountain-crowned city of Ashville, North Carolina.

Investing his portion of the family inheritance, George purchased an enormous tract of land in 1889 to build Biltmore Manor. He commissioned world-renowned architects and landscape designers to create an estate of distinction. The plans for the French Renaissance-style four-story mansion were modeled after three sixteenth century chateaux in Loire Valley, France.[9] Its construction required hundreds of local laborers and skilled artisans who handled countless tons of materials such as limestone, wood, and brick. A special railroad spur was built to transport materials to the site.

As the work progressed at home, George and his wife, Edith, traveled extensively throughout Europe to select artwork, tapestries, and furnishings to make the interior equally as impressive as the exterior. Six years later, in 1895, George Vanderbilt unveiled Biltmore Estates to his family and friends.

---

7. *Ibid*, P. 49
8. *Ibid*, P. 53
9. *The Biltmore*, P. 14

The carriage ride from the railroad station to the house was three miles, described as "magical miles"[10] of enchanting natural sights. The road design purposefully had no open views until, at the end, the forest opened up. There, the summit of a leveled mountain offered visages of the French Board River and the Swannanoa River with the Great Smoky Mountains rising in the background. As breathtaking as those views were, they were secondary to the sight of Biltmore Manor, the largest private residence built so far in the United States.

Sprawling with acres of floor space, the 250-room chateau featured a magnificent dining hall, 33 family and guest bedrooms, 43 bathrooms with indoor plumbing, 65 fireplaces, three kitchens, electricity, and an indoor swimming pool. The surreal grounds encompassed 125,000 acres of forest, farms, a dairy, a 250-acre wooded park, five manicured pleasure gardens, and 30 miles of navigable roads. The final price tag was about five million dollars, the equivalent of $180 million today.

Inside, the opulence of this "mountain retreat" was unparalleled with its worldly wealth on display. All of this was unveiled on Christmas Eve to the surprise of the family coming in from New York. They had no prior knowledge of the scope of the project and were utterly amazed at the ingenuity of young George, deeming him worthy of the name Vanderbilt.

The legacy of the Biltmore lives on as one of America's most celebrated tourist attractions. Nearby hotels house travelers who come to take in the history and splendor of the well-preserved mansion. A staff of eager volunteers help answer tourist's questions and self-guided tours using headphones aid visitors to browse the

10. *Fortune's Children*, P. 272

rooms at their own pace. The recorded dialogue they hear allows folks to step back in time to imagine daily life at the manor.

For anyone who has toured or seen pictures of Biltmore Estates, it is truly a mesmerizing "city on a hill." Yet, as exhilarating as those sights may be, they can't compare to the eternal "city on a hill," the New Jerusalem, described in the Book of Revelation. Here we look forward to what will be, instead of looking back at what was. **"For here we do not have an enduring city, but we are looking for the city that is to come." (Hebrews 13:14)**

Jesus put His followers at ease by telling them that He was going to a place to build them a future home with Him. **"Let not your heart be troubled; believe in God, believe also in Me. In My Father's house are many dwelling places; if it were not so, I would have told you; for I go to prepare a place for you." (John 14:1-2)** Just like George Vanderbilt who traveled to the scenic mountains of North Carolina to construct a retreat for family and friends, exclusively with their comfort in mind, so Jesus assures people of the same preparation. The Greek language translates "heavenly dwellings" as "mansions." Thus, it is appropriate to use the Biltmore as the visual for our eternal destiny.

Years after Christ ascended into heaven, the Apostle John described the city Jesus had built. John was caught up by the Holy Spirit in a futuristic vision while a prisoner on the Isle of Patmos and wrote about what he saw. **"And he carried me away in the Spirit to a great and high mountain and showed me the holy city from God having the glory of God, her brilliance was like a very costly stone, as a stone of crystal-clear jasper." (Revelation 21: 10-11)**

John cites the layout of the city as a square measuring 1,500 miles in length, width, and depth, figured in human measurements and angelic measurements. The brilliance of the materials Jesus used are beyond our comprehension. The city has no need of illumination from the sun or the moon because the glory of God provides its light. Interestingly, we will help decorate the facility by bringing the glory of our works for God with us when we get there.

Like the pure mountain waters flowing alongside the Biltmore, so the river of the water of life, clear as crystal, flows from God's throne. Along with the Tree of Life, this eternal water keeps everything and everyone vibrant and alive forevermore. **"And on either side of the river was the tree of life, bearing twelve kinds of fruit, yielding its fruit every month; and the leaves of the tree were for the healing of the nations." (Revelation 22:2)** Upon arrival, we will be healed of earth's disease, discomfort, and weakness. Our minds will be at perfect peace and our hearts will overflow with Joy. We will realize our forever freedom from planet earth's pain, trauma, and fears.

Most notably, we will co-exist with God Himself, never again to be separated from Him by sin. We will no longer suffer from the spector of death. Nor will we become bogged down and discouraged from the inglorious drudgery of life on earth.

Like turning the corner of that winding road to the Biltmore, the view of our future opens up when we read this description in Revelation. This is the place that Christ has prepared for those who put their hope in Him. How is this possible? We don't know and we won't know until we arrive there. But just like every home has a front door key to enter, the key that allows our entrance to the holy city is belief in God and in Jesus. Believe that this fantastic revelation is a true place. Convince yourself that what you read is ready and real.

Accept and internalize the teachings of Jesus as right, true, and worth following. Believe that Jesus is the resurrected Savior, sitting on heaven's throne, alive and capable of loving you right where you are. Realize that God, the ultimate Architect, will lead you on His righteous path towards Him until you reach your destination in His waiting, loving arms.

YOUR THOUGHTS

WHAT'S UNDER THE HOOD?

READ PSALM 139:1-6

*A*popular pastime for folks in our area and across the country is attending "Classic Car Shows" and "Cruise-Ins." These wholesome events attract car enthusiasts who drive their well-preserved older cars to a designated venue for public display. Local Facebook groups advertise the meeting time, date, and location on social media posts. Group organizers may arrange to use a shopping center, church, bar, or restaurant parking lot. A "Classic Car Show" may require registering the car and paying an entry fee. It also may feature contests and prizes. The "Cruise-Ins" are typically more impromptu. No reservations, no fees— just show up!

Either way, these gatherings offer a congenial atmosphere where people in the community can come out to view cars and chat with car owners who are casually seated in lawn chairs nearby. The owners look forward to answering questions about their vehicles.

Some of the car makes that may be featured are Corvette, Thunderbird, Challenger, Camaro, Mustang, or other "muscle" cars. Most of them have undergone some restoration to keep them running, although they may appear like new. Some rural groups feature their farm and garden tractors and equipment, to the delight of young children.

Most likely, a curious visitor will tap into the passion of the car owner by asking, "What's under the hood?" That person wants to know how fast the car was in its prime and what kind of performance the engine has. Other banter may arise as folks peer under the propped-up hood, asking questions about nostalgia, trivia, car manufacturing eras, road trips, chrome, accessories, and upkeep. Attendees come away with a feel-good time of meeting interesting people, exploring their hobby, and finding out facts about cool cars.

With this picture in mind, let's use the analogy of the car as the human body, the engine as the human heart, the steering wheel as our mind, and the fuel as our inner motives. Like car owners know their cars, we know ourselves. We know where we have been and where we wish to go. Our thought life has steered us to go places and say things all our lives.

Like the cars at the neighborhood car shows, we shouldn't just put on a show to impress others. God sees through our attempts to look good for others and keep our sin behind closed doors. Instead, like well-tuned engines, we should have our heart, mind and motives attuned to God's purposes.

In the Book of 1 Samuel, the prophet Samuel went to the house of Jesse as God directed him, to anoint one his sons as the next king of Israel. As each fine-looking young man passed by, the Lord disqualified each one. **"But the Lord said to Samuel, 'Do not look at his appearance or at the heights of his stature, because I have rejected him; for God sees not as man sees, for man looks at outward appearance, but the Lord looks at the heart.'" (1 Samuel 16:7)** Finally Jesse called his youngest son, David, in from tending sheep in the fields. The boy stood before Samuel with sun-tanned skin and beautiful eyes. **"Arise, anoint him; for this is he," the Lord said to Samuel. (1 Samuel 16: 9)** No one dreamed that the young shepherd would be chosen as king of Israel, but that is the mystery as God examines character within the heart.

Many years later, King David sings of God's ability to know him so well; better than he knew himself. He welcomes God's scrutiny and stands amazed at God's intimate knowledge of him. **"O Lord, Thou has searched me and know me. Thou dost know when I sit down and when I rise up, Thou dost understand my thoughts from afar. Thou dost scrutinize my path and my lying down, Thou art intimately acquainted with all my ways. Even before there is a word on my tongue, behold, O Lord, thou dost know it all." (Psalm 139: 1-6)**

Since an early age, King David knew that God watched his heart, just as God knows everyone's heart. At every moment, all over the world, God knows and sees all human hearts laid bare before Him, whether we realize it or not. That is the power of an omniscient God, who sees our thoughts before we form them into words. He scrutinizes our motives to keep us in check from ill-motivated actions. We should be glad that God sees us so completely. He knows us better than we know ourselves.

That is why we need to seek Him and ask Him "What is under my hood? What don't I see that I need to change?" That is the way to holiness. We are the only ones who can consciously decide to change our thoughts and actions to comply with God's correction.

King David again beseeches God concerning his heart. As an older man, weathered from war and kingdom intrigue, he wants that same innocence he once had as a young shepherd boy. **"Create in me a clean heart, O God, and renew a steadfast spirit in me." (Psalm 51:10)**

We are responsible to work in tandem with God's Spirit to discover and know our own heart, no matter what age, make, or model we are. Like the car owners sitting in lawn chairs waiting to chat, God will gladly tell us what we need to know about ourselves. That way, we can be true to ourselves and candid with others, living authentic lives_not just for show.

YOUR THOUGHTS

NEW LIFE IN THE CEMETARY

READ ACTS 5:14-20

O ur church owns and maintains a cemetery that was established over 100 years ago. Surrounding the sloping two-acre plot is a chain-link fence and lots of trees beyond that. Every year in June, a group of volunteers from our congregation come with rakes and work gloves to gather up the leaves that accumulate along the fence. We briskly rake them onto plastic tarps and haul them to the back of the church property, dumping them over a hill. This annual cemetery clean-up takes a couple of hours on a Saturday morning. I show up because I like the people and the exercise.

That morning, I briefly pulled away from raking to explore the monuments marking the graves of people who once lived. The oldest couple I found buried there was David and Katharyn Yoost. He was born in 1795 and died in 1871 after 74 years of living. She was born in 1805 and died in 1859 at a much younger age of 54. I started to wonder about them. How well did he do for those 20 years without her? Did they have a big family? What disease took her life so soon? Did he think about her every day and weep privately? I'll never know.

The most recent headstone I found was from 2013, marking the grave of the church organist. How old was she when she learned how to play the organ? Did she have a fulfilling career in music? Did the congregation appreciate her and turn out for her funeral? I won't know that either.

I kept strolling among the tombstones. I recognized the last names of people who had streets in the area named after them. Were they leaders in the community who sold off large tracts of land for subdivisions and shopping centers?

I noticed people who had fought in wars and were designated as revered veterans. One man fought in the War of 1812. Astounding! Other inscriptions were written in German, leaving me guessing what the family wanted to convey.

Finally, I spotted three rectangular brick-sized headstones. One was marked "Father," the next one, "Mother," and the next one "Baby." I flinched as I realized this couple had lost a child as a baby. How sad and unsettling. The grief that people face, as collectively represented by that graveyard, can be overwhelming.

Going back to raking with my group, a volunteer raised her voice for us to come look at something. Outside the fence was a fawn curled up and asleep in the shade of a large tree. There were no other deer in sight, but I was sure the mother would be back to take care of her baby.

Undisturbed by our presence, the baby deer slept peacefully. The scene offered some symbolism of new life as we worked within the bounds of the cemetery. Alongside a field of death was a baby deer ready to embark on its life adventure, living by its instincts to stay alive.

Here is my takeaway from the day. New life does not replace death, i.e., this one replaces that one. Nor does it come forth from death, as soil provides the substance for plants to sprout and grow. Instead, new life exists alongside death, like the fawn outside the cemetery. We have them both in this present age. When Jesus returns to earth, He will abolish death forever and we will have only life. Until then, we can have new life in the Spirit, the eternal life that God promises starts now.

This is how that is possible. The Bible tells of a man who lived among the tombs in a cemetery. He was painfully demon-possessed, crying, and cutting himself with stones. **"And constantly night and day, among the tombs and in the mountains, he was crying out and gashing himself with stones." (Mark 5:5)** The demons gave him no rest and drove away those who tried to help him.

When the man saw Jesus from a distance, he ran to Him. Jesus took authority over all the demons, for there were many, and cast them into a herd of pigs. The pigs reacted and rushed down a steep bank and drowned in the sea.

People of the town, who knew of the man living among the tombs, came out and saw Jesus with the man. He was calm, fully clothed and in his right mind because of Jesus. They were frightened from the incident and begged Jesus to leave. Before He left, Jesus told the healed man to tell people about the new life that God gave him.

Later in Church history after Jesus ascended into heaven, the Apostles were performing miraculous healings in Jesus' name. The Sadducees were jealous of them as the crowd brought sick people to them to be healed. Those religious leaders had the Apostles arrested and thrown in jail. During the night, the Lord sent an angel to unlock the prison doors to release them. **"But an angel of the Lord during the night opened the gates of the prison, and taking them out he said, 'Go your way, stand and speak to the people in the temple the whole message of this new life."** (Acts 5:19-20)

Here is the full message of the new life of which the angel spoke. Like the demon-possessed man, a life of sin is a dark, difficult, unhappy way to live. Seeing Jesus and running to Him as Savior removes us from our bondage to sin. The realm on earth called "new life" is afforded by Jesus and energized by the Holy Spirit. Jesus administers heaven's help and healing in His name. **"That which is born of the flesh is flesh; and that which is born of the Spirit is spirit. Do not marvel that I said to you 'You must be born again.'"** (John 3:6-7)

How can we have the "new life" that Jesus makes possible? This blessing from God comes when you stop trusting solely in yourself, have faith in Jesus, renounce your sin, and ask Him to take control of your life. He will do that with His Spirit. You can be "born-again" into God's realm of eternal life now and forever.

Like those monuments rising from the cemetery grounds, there are three pillars of new life, ageless as those granite stones: 1) Desire God to speak to you, 2) Hear what He tells you and 3) Do what He says. If you live with these three pillars in place, you will cross over from death and, like the baby deer resting quietly, be on the side of life.

YOUR THOUGHTS

3D GLASSES

READ EPHESIANS 1:15-21

*D*oes anyone remember wearing 3D glasses as a kid? The frames are normally made of cardboard holding one plastic lens that is vivid red and another lens that is vibrant blue. Peering through them, the eyes send two separate images to the brain. The brain is essentially tricked into combining the two images into one, projecting a layer of dimension to the object it sees. Instead of just perceiving the height and width of an object, the eyes see an added dimension of breadth, hence the 3D quality of a third dimension.[11] People wear these trick glasses to enhance their movie or television

---

11. *All About Vision*

entertainment. The third dimension increases the viewing pleasure with a more life-like picture.

Like wearing 3D glasses, believers who receive the Holy Spirit into their lives experience heaven as an added dimension to their reality. During a clandestine meeting with Nicodemus, Jesus explained the reality of the Holy Spirit to this teacher of the law. **"Jesus answered, 'Truly, truly I say to you, unless one is born of water and the Spirit, he cannot enter into the kingdom of God...the wind blows wherever it wishes...so is everyone who is born of the Spirit.'" (John 3:5-8)**

Christianity was about to take a turn, no longer to just be about the printed page of the Law, flat and two dimensional. The spiritual life will consist of the written Word of God enlivened by interaction with the Spirit of God. The "blowing wind" that Jesus spoke of will be believers directed and empowered by the Spirit.

That new type of life began with the entrance of the Holy Spirit onto Jesus as recorded in Matthew 3:16-17. **"And after being baptized, Jesus went up immediately from the water, and behold the heavens were opened and He saw the Spirit of God descending as a dove, and coming upon Him, and behold, a voice out of the heavens, saying, 'This is My beloved Son, in whom I am well pleased.'" (Matthew 3: 16-17)** God the Son emerged from His water baptism by John the Baptist, was met by God the Spirit, and endorsed by God the Father.

Movie depictions of this scene show a fluttering white dove alighting on Jesus' shoulder. That is an innocuous interpretation that merely represents the utmost gentleness of the Spirit. Actually, the heavens tore open, releasing the all-powerful Agent of creation onto the human body of Jesus. If the Spirit had not landed gently, He would have knocked Jesus over. Also, the voice of God the Father was equally measured. If His voice had been full capacity, it would have crushed creation. Empowered now by the Holy Spirit, Jesus would do the miracle ministry that He was sent to do. In fact, the Apostle John notes that all of Jesus' miracles were not recorded because they were too numerous to write down.

Jesus was well-equipped to be the new prototype of man, the "last Adam," **"born of water and born of the Spirit." (John 3:5)** This was the inception of a new race of man that would be born of natural patents and born-again by God. Jesus lived by the power of the Spirit for the remainder of His life as an example of how we should also live. Living by God's power rather than our own is the added dimension we have, as modeled by Jesus.

After His crucifixion and resurrection, Jesus told the Disciples that this same Holy Spirit was going to descend upon them. He would send the Spirit to them after He ascended to heaven. **"...but you shall receive power when the Holy Spirit has come upon you..." (Acts 1:8)** The arrival of the Holy Spirit took place on the day of Pentecost as the believers were gathered in an upper room. **"And when the day of Pentecost had come, they were all together in one place. And suddenly there came from heaven a noise like a violent, rushing wind...and they were all filled with the Holy Spirit and began to speak in other tongues, as the Spirit was giving them utterance. "(Acts 2: 1-4)**

Since then, the presence of the Holy Spirit adds a new dimension to believers' lives, making them aware of God, to commune with Him and understand the words of the Bible. Daily living in this dimension is called "walking by the Spirit." **"But I say, walk by the Spirit and you will not carry out the desires of the flesh."** (Galatians 5:16)

In this way, we have the power to hold ourselves back from acting on dark, base instincts. The Bible trains our mind to know God's distinction between right and wrong. Even greater than those Christian basics, we can have a vision for our lives and some idea of our future. As we follow the direction of the Holy Spirit, we can sense when we arrive at the right place, at the right time.

Our life unfolds in a unique and profound way because we have heaven's perspective. Not only do we see the world differently, but we also see ourselves differently for the better. Bolstered by the awareness and backing of God, we focus more on what we *can* do rather than being held back by what we *can't* do.

In his book, *Living In The Spirit*, Assemblies of God general superintendent Dr. George O. Wood makes these remarks about people who walk in the Spirit. "Second, the Spirit taps the potential in our life that no one or nothing else can reach. No single person's life is ever the same after having encountered the Holy Spirit...No matter how much energy we bring to any particular assignment or task, only the Holy Spirit can touch the depths of potential in our life and draw them forth for the Kingdom of God."[12] Additionally, the supernatural quality of life in the Spirit propels us beyond our own natural abilities, not in a "magical" sense, but by having heaven's reality present with us.

---

12. *Living In The Spirit*, PP 42-43

It was the Apostle Paul's urgent prayer that believers understand and accept the supernatural dimension of life in the Spirit. **"I pray that the eyes of your heart may be enlightened, so that you may know what is the hope of His calling, what are the riches of the glory of His inheritance in the saints and what is the surpassing greatness of His power towards us who believe." (Ephesians 1:18-19)** With 3D glasses we can see a third dimension with our eyes that is not real. But with the Holy Spirit, we can see the reality of heaven's riches with the eyes of our heart.

YOUR THOUGHTS

SEAMLESS

READ JOHN 14:6-11

*L*ike the beginning of this book, our stories end with the visual of an immense cloudless sky reflecting down on calm lake waters below. That was our vista stretching for miles on a day at the beach. My husband and I made a trip with a friend and her two young adult children to Mentor Headlands State Park, a well-maintained beach and picnic area on the Ohio shores of Lake Erie. We relished the clear day, the mild lake breeze, and the air temperature in the mid-80s. The water temperature was much colder because there were few hot days to warm up the lake by mid-June.

We piled out of the car and grabbed our towels and belongings. Just beyond the parking lot and past the concession stand was a blue mesh walkway fastened into the sandy ground by stakes. It paved the way for beachgoers to access the water more easily without trudging through sand, spanning the beach like a runway. Following that sightline and looking up, we could barely discern where the water ended, and the blue sky began. The horizon between the lake and sky was seamless.

Donning our sunhats and sunglasses, we went down to the water wearing flip-flop sandals. Barry watched as the rest of us waded into the water calf deep. We squealed as the chilly waves broke over us. Twice, the incessant waves snatched flip-flops from our toes, sending us scrambling in the sinking sand to rescue them. The ebb and flow of the water was formidable, cautioning us not to wade out any further.

We exited the water and dried our feet with beach towels, working the corners of them in between our toes to remove the itchy sand. Barry and the kids moved their activities to land, tossing a wobbly Frisbee between them. The lake breeze chose to play and have its own way with their plastic toy.

The morning flew past, and we traveled back up the walkway to retrieve the coolers to have lunch. We found a picnic table that didn't have too many wooden splinters on the seat and unfurled a plastic tablecloth to cover the top. I handed out the sandwiches we packed: turkey breast and Swiss cheese on flaky croissant rolls, pickles, and some yellow mustard. We also packed some cut-up vegetables, fruit, Rice-Krispie treats, oatmeal cookies, and a bag of potato chips. The lake breeze intervened again, tousling our hair as we bowed our heads to say "grace," thanking God for our ample luncheon. As we chatted quietly, we could hear the waves breaking in the distance along the shore. There was something about the boundlessness of nature that reminded us that God is big, and we are not. Refreshed and with our minds reset, we packed everything up and drove our drowsy sun-drenched self's home.

Barry and I were glad we spent the day with our friends, realizing how much we needed to be with them. We had considered canceling because, two days prior, we put down his 15-year-old dog, Livy. Spending the day with them helped take the edge off our grief.

The dog had suffered a stroke about two months earlier and we noticed her health deteriorating. Barry reluctantly made the vet appointment to put her down. That day, he boosted her into the back seat of the car for a long, quiet trip. He lifted her from the car and carried her into the vet office. The sympathetic receptionist took us into a low-lit room where they put pets "to sleep." We both sat sobbing, looking down at Livy and saying our last "goodbyes." Our bodies shook with emotion.

The veterinary staff member came into the room and quietly approached us. She was crying, too.

"I am so sorry you are losing a friend today," she said genuinely. "This is the fifth animal we are losing today and none of them are easy." Her empathy warmed us, and we knew we were not alone going through this emotional experience. The vet came in and administered the euthanizing solution and in less than a minute, Livy was gone from us, painlessly passing on to another realm.

The next day, Barry and I attended the wake for his co-worker's father who passed away. We were still hurting from losing Livy, so we understood in a fresh way the loss of a family member.

"We are so sorry for your loss," I said to his mother, searching for words of condolence. Her eyes filled with fresh tears as she nodded to us and glanced across the room to the motionless body of her husband of 50 years. Barry and I held hands, feeling the warm touch between us and knowing it was not forever. We walked around the perimeter of the funeral home room, examining family photos glued to poster boards. All the stages of their family were captured in the photos on display. We saw the parents proudly holding their newborn children and all the events leading up to them holding their grandchildren. For the moment, we stood with this family and celebrated their lives together. Death could not steal the memories they made as a family.

Like those chilly lake waters breaking over us, here we stood experiencing the ebb and flow of everyday human life. What a comfort to know that no one understands us like Jesus. One day our hearts were breaking from losing our dog and two days later we were freely roaming the beach. One day we may be gazing into the eyes of a loved one, carrying on a normal conversation, and soon enough we are closing their eyes for the last time. With the interplay of all our emotions, Jesus is with us during the highs, the lows, and everything in between. Who else keeps track of our complexities and closely monitors our hearts?

Only Him. Why? Because, like that beach walkway leading out to the endless horizon, Jesus Christ stands as the seamless God-Man. He is fully God and fully Man, understanding our weakness and appealing to God on our behalf. **"I am the way, the truth and the Life. Not one comes to the Father except through Me."** (John 14:6)

Jesus IS the reflection of heaven on earth. He is the embodiment of the sun, the moon, and all facets of creation. Born as an ordinary man, He lived an extraordinary, heaven-empowered life and now He lives, making intercession for us non-stop. With Him, we can live extraordinary lives also.

As you consider these parables and choose to align yourself with heaven, you will become like Him. And as you live in Him, and He in you, living that seamless life together, people will take notice and see heaven on planet earth...in you.

YOUR THOUGHTS

PRAYER TO RECEIVE JESUS CHRIST AS SAVIOR

DEAR JESUS,

I BELIEVE THAT YOU ARE THE SON OF GOD. I BELIEVE THAT YOU CAME TO EARTH AND DIED ON A CROSS TO PAY FOR THE SINS OF THE WHOLE WORLD. I BELIEVE YOU WERE RAISED FROM THE DEAD AND YOU ARE NOW SEATED IN HEAVEN.

I ADMIT THAT I AM A SINNER BEFORE YOU AND I AM WILLING TO CHANGE. I WANT TO TURN AWAY FROM MY SIN AND TURN TO YOU. I AM SORRY, PLEASE FORGIVE ME.

NOW, JESUS, I ASK YOU TO COME INTO MY LIFE AND TAKE FULL CONTROL. PLEASE SHOW ME HOW TO LIVE A LIFE THAT IS PLEASING TO GOD. THANK YOU. AMEN

If you have spoken this prayer to God for the first time, then believe that He has heard you and now has relationship with you. Continue in relationship with Him through Bible reading, prayer, and church attendance. He will fill you with the assurance of the indwelling Holy Spirit and you will experience His life and His love. God bless you.

RESOURCES

Alcorn, Randy, _Heaven_, 2004, Tyndale House Publishers, Inc., Carol Stream, IL

Boice, James Montgomery, _The Parables of Jesus_, 1983, Moody Press, Chicago, IL

Cecil, Bill Jr., _Biltmore, An American Masterpiece_, 2o12, The Biltmore Company, Asheville, NC

Guthrie, D., _The New Bible Commentary Revised_, 1970, Intervarsity Press, Leicester, England

Mains, David, _Thy Kingship Come_, 1989, Zondervan Books, Grand Rapids, MI

Sherman, Casey and Wedge, David, _Boston Strong_, 2015, University Press, Lebanon, NH

Snodgrass, Klyne R., _Stories With Intent_, 2008 Wm. B. Eerdmans Publishing Co., Grand Rapids, MI

Sproul, R. C., _What do Jesus' Parables Mean?_, 2017 Reformation Trust Publishing, Sanford, FL

Vanderbilt, Aurthur T., Fortune's Children, 1989, William Morrow and Company, New York, NY

Wood, George O., _Living In The Spirit_, 2009, Gospel Publishing House, Springfield, MI

INTERNET ARTICLES

Birding Hotspots, Hinckley Reservation Website

Ohio Traveler by Robert Carpenter

CNN Sports "Gigantic Alligator Spotted Roaming Florida Golf Course," by Ben Morse

What Alligators Eat

Newsweek "Watch Alligator" by Hanah Osborne

People Magazine, January 30, 2023

Entertainment, Lisa Marie Presley by Brianne Tracy

Insider, Lisa Marie Wrote About Grief, by Eve Crosbie

OTHER BOOKS BY DIANE EHRLICH

Available through www.amazon.com

OR

www.reformministry.com

 TRANSFORMING THE QUEEN

 TAKE THE LIMITS OFF OF GOD!

 SEEING BEHIND THE MASK

 TABERNACLE—PROTECTING THE PRESENCE OF GOD

CONFIDENCE SHALL BE YOUR STRENGTH!

 RECIPE FOR SHARING

 HOW TO WRITE A BOOK